TEA GARDENING FOR BEGINNERS

tea gardening for beginners

Learn to Grow, Blend, and Brew Your Own Tea at Home

JULIA DIMAKOS

Illustrations by Ellen Korbonski

To my husband, Stelios, who has always supported my dreams, and my sister-in-law Dini, who encouraged me to share my knowledge and passion for growing food.

First Rockridge Press trade paperback edition 2022

For general information on our other products and services, please contact our Customer Care Department within the United States at (866) 744-2665, or outside the United States at (510) 253-0500.

Paperback ISBN: 978-1-63878-573-6 | eBook ISBN: 978-1-63878-710-5

Manufactured in the United States of America

Interior and Cover Designer: Sean Doyle
Art Producer: Janice Ackerman
Editor: Anne Lowrey
Production Editor: Caroline Flanagan
Production Manager: Riley Hoffman

Illustration: © 2022 Ellen Korbonski
Author photo courtesy of Jamie Spurrell

10 9 8 7 6 5 4 3 2 1 0

Contents

Introduction

When I first started growing food eleven years ago, the sole purpose was to feed my family healthy, organic vegetables. I grew everything I could, squished into a four-foot-by-sixteen-foot bed. Some things did well, like tomatoes, and three massive zucchini plants overran others. It was an eye-opener for me, and the vegetables tasted better than anything store-bought.

I learned a lot in that first year, and my passion for gardening grew. Each year, I tried growing something new in the vegetable garden, expanding from popular vegetables to more unusual varieties while growing herbs and berries.

After moving to the country, then expanding our kitchen garden from two thousand to seven thousand square feet, I had to grow more. I thought, if I could grow vegetables and herbs, I could grow my own tea garden. So, I tasted a lot of herbal tea blends, investigated ingredients, and realized that, yes, I could grow most of them myself.

Although I love green and black tea, my climate and hardiness zone are not conducive to growing the tea plant, *Camellia sinensis*. But the sky is the limit with herbs, and many have no trouble growing in my northern climate. Some herbs are perennial and grow back year after year; the ones that won't overwinter have enough time to produce a crop before the end of the growing season.

I've grown many herbs over the years and learned what does well and what needs extra time to produce a crop. A couple of my favorites are lemongrass and roselle (hibiscus). Each has a very long growing season, and if started in January, it will grow to maturity. I learned how many plants I needed to produce a decent-size harvest by experimenting.

In this book, I will give you all the tools you need to grow your own tea garden. I will discuss the history of tea and the one plant that produces all true tea, *Camellia sinensis*. I will identify the differences between black, green, white, and oolong tea. If you live in a warm climate, you will learn how to grow your own tea plants and when to harvest them.

If your climate isn't warm enough to grow the tea plant, you'll read about thirty-six herb plants that make a wonderful brew. Many of these herbs have dual purposes and can also be used in culinary recipes. I give you guidelines on how to grow these plants, then craft and brew your own tea blends. At the end, there are ten recipes to get you started blending and brewing your own delicious teas.

It's all covered in this book: everything you need from tools to watering, soil, plant care, garden types, growing from seed, garden plans, and more. All the ideas in these pages will give you a foundation for designing, planning, and growing your own tea garden.

And once your herb plants grow, I will teach you how best to harvest and preserve them, the correct temperature at which to brew them, and how best to make your own fragrant and satisfying homegrown teas.

CHAPTER 1

What Is Tea?

All tea comes from one source, the plant known as *Camellia sinensis*. Knowing when to harvest and the correct way to process its leaves will determine whether you enjoy green, white, black, or oolong tea.

In this chapter, I'll discuss the history of the tea plant, the four different teas, their characteristics, and steeping techniques, as well as harvesting and processing methods.

Herbal tisanes use the leaves, flowers, fruit, seeds, and roots of herbs, and I'll explain how you can use these plant parts to craft and brew your own herbal tea blends. Store-bought tea simply does not compare to homegrown freshness. Once I show you the benefits, you will want to grow your own.

Camellia Sinensis—The Source of All Tea

Whether black, green, white, or oolong, all teas come from one evergreen plant, *Camellia sinensis*. Originating in the Yunnan and Sichuan provinces of southern China, only two main varieties of the camellia plant are harvested from to make tea: *Camellia sinensis* var. *sinensis* and *Camellia sinensis* var. *assamica*. We can refer to it as the tea bush for ease of identification.

Legend has it that in 2737 BCE, the Chinese emperor Shen Nung sat beneath a *Camellia sinensis* tree, sipping boiling water. Suddenly a few leaves blew off the tree and into the pot. Because Shen Nung was an herbalist, he decided to allow the leaves to brew, to see what would happen. He enjoyed the resulting flavor, and from there, tea started its journey through time.

Tea has been prevalent in China for centuries, and much has been written about it. For hundreds of years, tea was imported from China to Europe until the East India Company began growing tea in Assam, India. In 1858, the British government took control of the East India Company after the camellia plants had been established and spread throughout the region. From there, tea imports expanded into Britain, and by 1901, tea was deeply entrenched in everyday life.

Types of Tea

Camellia sinensis is a fascinating plant because of its ability to produce all true tea. After harvesting leaves from the tea bush, it is important to begin the oxidation and preserving process immediately. Each tea has its own preservation method, which will determine whether the resulting tea is white, green, black, or oolong. Delaying processing negatively affects the quality of the resulting tea and its storability.

Oxidation occurs when harvested tea leaves are exposed to air, which causes them to dry and darken in color like apples or potatoes darken when sliced. Oxidation determines the tea type, including flavor and aroma.

White tea is harvested in the spring and usually over a two-week period. It is important to keep an eye on the plants during this time and harvest while the leaf buds are still tightly bound. Bud tips are downy soft, whitish-gray, and produce a tea with a delicate aroma and subtly sweet flavor. Overdrying of the leaf buds will spoil the resulting tea. White tea is mildly oxidized.

Green tea is harvested in the spring after the tea bush comes out of winter dormancy. Once the plant produces new leaves, pick the top two leaves and the leaf bud. The leaves will be bright green and tender, growing on light green stems. When infused, green tea has a greenish color and goes through minimal oxidation to preserve it.

Black tea is typically harvested from *Camellia sinensis* var. *assamica* for its larger leaf size. However, if you only have one *Camellia sinensis* variety, you may still make black tea from the leaves. For black tea, harvest the top two leaves and the bud. The resulting infusion tends to have a golden brown to dark brown color due to the leaves being fully oxidized.

Oolong tea is not as dark as black tea but is darker than green. This tea falls nicely between black and green tea in flavor profile and strength. For this tea, harvest the top three leaves and the leaf bud. Oxidation level varies considerably for each variety of oolong.

All teas of the *Camellia sinensis* plant contain caffeine. Tea made from the leaf tips and buds has higher levels of caffeine than older leaves farther down the stem. This is because the plant uses caffeine to repel insects. To reduce caffeine intake, consider brewing fewer leaves per cup, brewing at a lower temperature, and reducing the steep time.

White Tea

White tea comes from the delicate leaf bud tips of the tea plant. The soft white hairs on the buds are the reason white tea got its name. Each stem produces only one leaf bud, so time and care are needed to carefully pluck each bud by hand to preserve as many whitish hairs as possible. On a large plantation, it would take many skilled employees to work through the plants, plucking the buds without damaging them. For this reason, white tea is pricier than most other teas.

Climate is the most important consideration for the ideal production of white tea. Since the late 1700s, some of the best white teas have come from the Fujian province in China. The mountainous countryside provides optimal temperature conditions for the plants to grow slowly, store natural sugars from the soil, and develop flavor compounds. It is possible to grow white tea in other environments, but the flavor will differ from tea grown in its natural terroir.

White tea is naturally high in antioxidants and has been shown to help maintain healthy teeth, assist with weight loss, and reduce the risk of heart disease.

FLAVOR PROFILE

White tea has a delicate, sweet aroma and ranges in flavor from refreshing and mildly sweet to grassy or nutty. The final flavor is based on the chosen oxidation process and drying method.

In Fujian, where the tea originated, some processing facilities dry the leaves in the traditional manner, first on large bamboo trays, then outside in the sun. Other facilities use large conveyor belts and computers to operate the machines. Each method is controlled, and each one results in a different tasting tea.

STEEPING

Water temperature affects the final flavor of white tea. Steeping at a low temperature, between 175°F and 185°F (80°C to 85°C), will result in a floral and fruity flavor. You may notice hints of mango, melon, or grassy notes. If the tea is steeped at a higher temperature of 195°F to 205°F (90°C to 95°C), you may notice a more nutty, woodsy flavor.

Although all flavors are pleasant, you will have your personal preference. Steep the tea until the tea leaves begin to drop in the pot (three or four minutes) and experiment with different temperatures.

BLENDS BEST WITH . . .

If you are brewing a white tea from Fujian, I wouldn't recommend blending it with anything. Take the opportunity to enjoy this tea on its own.

If you have white tea in tea bags or a loose-leaf packet with broken bits, both products will be of similar quality and could easily be blended with other ingredients. Because white tea has subtle fruity or floral aromas, consider adding dry fruit or flowers to the tea. Adding a few pieces of chopped dry pineapple or mango would bring out the fruity notes. Adding rose petals would bring out the floral notes.

Green Tea

Green tea has been produced in China and Japan for thousands of years, and each country has its own processing method. To preserve the fresh green color of the tea leaves, the oxidation process needs to be stopped immediately upon harvest. This is done with heat. In Japan, the leaves are steamed to halt oxidation, whereas in China, they are "panned" in large vessels that resemble woks. Of the four tea types, green is the only one that is not allowed to oxidize, as this would greatly damage the leaves and resulting flavor.

After heating, the leaves are rolled and shaped into many of the varieties available. Some popular varieties include sencha, jasmine, gunpowder, and genmaicha. Each has its own processing method, which results in its own unique flavor.

Green tea contains the highest levels of antioxidants, along with polyphenolic molecules called catechins, which have certain anticancer abilities. Green tea has more catechins than other teas because the tea leaves are not exposed to oxidation, thereby preserving the molecules within each leaf. If you want to grow your own tea, green tea is easier to process than the others.

FLAVOR PROFILE

The flavor of green tea can be described as floral, sweet, nutty, or vegetal. Before green tea was consumed for tea, it was eaten as soup. Today, when tea leaves are steamed during processing, many savory umami elements can be extracted from them.

When green tea is brewed at a high temperature, the catechins present in the leaf will release an astringent flavor. If you experienced bitterness when drinking green tea, the temperature of the water was too high. To prevent this and experience the best flavor elements, brew green tea at a temperature around 175°F (80°C).

STEEPING

Green tea is best steeped for less than a minute and at a low temperature of 175°F to 185°F (80°C to 85°C). By brewing for a shorter time, you release less caffeine and extract softer, more delicate tea notes.

Shorter brews will produce teas with a mild flavor. Over-steeping creates a richer-tasting tea. Either length of time is acceptable if the brew temperature is low. After steeping, drain all the tea into a cup, then feel free to steep the leaves a second and third time and adjust the brew length. Each steep will extract new flavor notes.

BLENDS BEST WITH . . .

The floral and fruity notes in green tea blend well with plants or ingredients that match. Choose a loose-leaf or bagged green tea, then pair it with lavender or jasmine. Add 1 teaspoon of lavender or jasmine petals to a small pot, along with 1 teaspoon of green tea. Steep at 175°F for one or two minutes.

Green tea also blends well with fresh mint leaves. Add 1 tablespoon of fresh mint or 1 teaspoon of dried mint to the blend. To bring out fruity notes, add a slice of lemon or dry lemon peel or sliced strawberries; the flavors will complement one another. Browse the tea aisle for ideas.

Black Tea

Black tea is the most popular and widely consumed beverage. It is well known that British people love their black tea. It may be enjoyed hot or iced, and images and feelings of comfort and coziness come to mind when we think of having a cuppa.

Some well-known black teas include Earl Grey, Ceylon, Assam, and Darjeeling. Unlike other teas, black teas are grown and processed around the world. Some of the larger productions can be found in China, India, Sri Lanka, and Africa. In these environments, the tea bushes grow in their optimal heat and humidity conditions.

Black tea is the only tea type with completely oxidized leaves. Leaves are left to oxidize for up to twelve hours after being withered and rolled. Rolling the leaves breaks down cell walls, releasing enzymes and triggering oxidation. Sometimes the leaves start turning brown during rolling, or the change happens as they oxidize. After the oxidation process is complete, the leaves will have changed from green to dark brown.

It is during this process that the flavor of black tea emerges. To complete the process, leaves are laid out in a warm environment where they develop notes of sweetness or earthiness.

FLAVOR PROFILE

Depending on the temperature of the brew, black tea will release different flavor profiles. When black tea is brewed at a lower temperature (175°F to 185°F), the flavors will be sweeter, fruitier, and lighter. The finish will also be softer on the palate.

When black tea is brewed at a higher temperature (195°F to 210°F), the flavors will be deeper, more malty, woody, spicier, and potentially more bitter. The liquid will seem thicker and richer, too. Milk pairs well with black tea brewed at a higher temperature and is satisfying to many people.

The color of black tea changes with the brew temperature. The lower the temperature, the lighter the color, whereas the higher the temperature, the darker the liquid. The caffeine content changes, too, increasing the longer the leaves are steeped.

STEEPING

Because black tea is a dark tea leaf, the length of steeping will affect the flavor profile, strength, and color of the resulting tea. With loose-leaf tea, feel free to experiment. Steep 1 teaspoon, followed by 1 tablespoon. Also, experiment with the steep time. Start with thirty seconds and move up to two minutes. The longer the steep, the deeper the flavor. Taste the tea and decide on your preference.

The quantity of tea is usually lower in store-bought tea bags. It is also difficult to know the quality of the tea, as tea bags usually contain broken pieces. Steep this tea for up to two minutes, then remove the tea bag to prevent over-steeping.

BLENDS BEST WITH . . .

The fruity notes of black tea pair well with dry fruit such as strawberries and blueberries. Citrus also pairs well with black tea. Add dry orange, lemon peel, or a slice of fresh lemon to lighten and brighten the tea.

Because black tea has sweet, malty notes, adding vanilla extract or vanilla bean to the brew will create a rich and satisfying tea. Cocoa and cinnamon also blend well and help balance out the rich flavors. Black tea has floral notes that come forward when blended with lavender buds or rose petals. Consider the flavor notes you are trying to extract and choose the pairings accordingly.

Oolong Tea

Oolong tea falls between green and black tea in strength, flavor, and color. Unlike other teas, oolong teas are semi-oxidized. Some producers oxidize the leaves until they reach a level of 10 to 45 percent, whereas others stop when the leaves reach 45 to 85 percent. This wide range is responsible for a broad palette of flavors and aromas in oolong tea.

The lower oxidized teas resemble green tea, whereas the higher oxidized teas are similar to black tea. The teas in the middle will have their own unique flavor. Each grower produces their own oolong, and the range of flavors is vast.

Oolong production first began in the 1600s in China, when tea growers started semi-oxidizing the leaves. Today, oolong teas are primarily grown and produced in China and Taiwan. Leaves are rolled before being oxidized, which is different from the usual method of oxidizing then rolling. Each producer has their own technique, resulting in their own unique oolong tea. There are many health benefits to drinking oolong tea, such as reduced LDL ("bad") cholesterol, lower blood pressure, and the prevention of cavities, to name a few.

FLAVOR PROFILE

It is difficult to describe oolong teas in simple terms because the flavors change based on the percentage of oxidation in the leaves. Less-oxidized oolongs tend to have a fruity, floral, or vegetal flavor. You may notice hints of jasmine, lilac, or orange blossom when drinking. Elements of strawberry, peach, or grape might come through. More-oxidized oolongs tend to have a richer flavor. You might notice notes of spice and confectionery, such as caramel, vanilla, cinnamon, and nutmeg, along with browned butter, milk, and cream. The range in flavor is quite interesting, making oolong tea fun to explore.

STEEPING

There is no hard-and-fast rule for steeping oolong teas. You want to brew oolong at a higher temperature, just below the boiling point. I recommend brewing at 195°F to 205°F (90°C to 97°C) for the best flavor. Brew for one or two minutes, then strain the tea into a cup.

Oolong tea can be steeped seven to ten times; each time will extract new flavors. Try brewing it in different ways. One approach is to do a short steep the first steep, adding ten seconds with each steep. You can also steep in reverse: longer for the first steep, then reduced by ten seconds for each subsequent steep.

BLENDS BEST WITH . . .

The lighter-colored oolong leaves are less oxidized, whereas darker oolongs tend to be more oxidized. Keep that in mind when you choose the pairings based on the flavor notes of each tea.

Lighter oolongs will blend well with fruity ingredients such as melon, peach, ginger, and lemon. Blend darker oolongs with cinnamon, cocoa, and cardamom to bring out the spicy notes. When brewing the tea, you may even add a small amount of vanilla extract or a slice of vanilla bean to complement the confectionary notes. Consider blending white tea with oolong, as the two pair well together.

THE HISTORY OF GROWING TEA

Tea was grown and consumed in China for thousands of years before being introduced to the wider world. Originally, tea was unknown as a beverage. People used the leaves as a flavoring for meals, adding them to other ingredients. It was also regarded as a medicinal plant because it supplied many vitamins to the simple diets of the native people.

Processing methods changed significantly over the centuries, adapting to each dynasty change. In the fourth and fifth centuries, spices, onions, rice, salt, and other ingredients were added to tea. Before the regular population enjoyed tea, it was reserved for emperors and high-ranking officials. It wasn't until the Tang dynasty (618–907 CE) that tea was boiled. Finally, during the Ming dynasty in the 1300s, tea was first infused using the process we follow now. Today, tea is the second most consumed beverage in the world, behind only water.

Tea harvesting methods have remained consistent throughout history. Skilled pickers plucked leaves manually to preserve as many of the aromatics as possible. Although some operations use machines for harvesting, this is not efficient on steep terrains and slopes. For this reason, manual leaf-by-leaf harvesting continues.

Herbal Teas (Tisanes)

Unlike teas using the *Camellia sinensis* plant, herbal teas are steeped with herbs. Different parts of the plant—such as leaves, flowers, fruit, seeds, and roots—can be used when making teas. Each ingredient imparts its own flavor. By combining or blending several herbs, you can create your own herbal tea blends. Although some herbs are better suited for culinary purposes, here I am referring to herbs suitable for steeping.

Tisane is a word used to describe herbal teas. When we describe tea as a tisane, we identify that the blend consists solely of herbal ingredients and not leaves of the *Camellia sinensis* plant. It is important to categorize herbal teas as tisanes to identify that these teas are caffeine-free. Some familiar tisanes include chamomile and mint tea. Lemon and other fruity teas are also popular, and they tend to contain ingredients such as hibiscus (roselle), dried fruit, lemon peel, lemongrass, and others.

Because many herbs also have medicinal properties, it is important to know the ingredients of your tea blends and how they may affect you. Be sure to monitor for potential allergies and check for possible contraindications with any medications you may be taking.

Leaves

Leaves are the green vegetative parts of herb plants. Harvest fresh, undamaged leaves from the upper half of the plant, because lower leaves are older and lower in quality. Fresh leaves have a bright, vegetative flavor. I have experienced notes of bitterness with some and citrus with others. When leaves are dried, they develop deeper and more complex flavors. Depending on the herb, the flavor may change entirely.

To steep, measure at least one tablespoon of fresh or one teaspoon of dried leaf and cover with boiling water (195°F to 205°F). Steep for at least three or four minutes. The longer the steep, the stronger the flavor.

Flowers

A tea of flowers can provide many wonderful benefits. Flowers add floral elements and aromas to tea. They also add color and aesthetic appeal. Some flowers are potent enough to be brewed on their own. Chamomile, for example, has a strong flavor and a calming effect when steeped. Lavender also has a wonderful relaxing aroma, but it may be too strong on its own and is better blended with other flowers or ingredients. It is best to steep flowers for at least four or five minutes in boiling water (195°F to 205°F). The longer the steep, the more flavorful the tea.

Fruits and Seeds

Fruits and seeds may be steeped on their own or blended with other herbal ingredients. Lemon is pungent and, on its own, makes a very flavorful tea. Fennel seeds make a soothing tea for the stomach, especially after a heavy meal. When ingredients have a strong aroma, they don't require blending. However, mild-tasting fruit such as rosehips, goji berry, and black currants benefit when paired with another ingredient that helps bring out a depth of flavor. Steep fruits and seeds in boiled water (195°F to 205°F) for at least four or five minutes or longer to release all their flavors and aromatics.

Roots

Some plants, such as ginger, licorice, and dandelion, are better used for their roots rather than their leaves. Although the leaves of these plants are edible, for the purposes of tea, more benefit will come from the roots.

To prepare herbal roots, boil them in a saucepan to extract their flavors and health benefits. Boil water at 195°F to 205°F for at least five to fifteen minutes, depending on the root, then strain into a cup. Roots may be boiled several times. Note that roots have a deep flavor and can become bitter if overcooked.

Crafting Mindful Blends

Blends tend to have three parts: base ingredient, secondary ingredient, and accent ingredients. When creating a tea blend, think about the recipe in these three components.

The base ingredients have a strong flavor and make up the bulk of the tea blend. Examples include mint, chamomile, and anise. The simplest way to measure out herbs is in parts. Choose a measuring tool and use it consistently throughout. I like to use a tablespoon for small portions. Measure three tablespoons or three parts of the base ingredient.

Next, select the secondary ingredient. These ingredients help round out and balance the base ingredients. Some herbal examples include roselle, rosehips, and lemon balm, which are very simple to grow in a tea garden, so choose and plant several secondary ingredients. For secondary ingredients, measure out two parts.

The accent ingredients add a finishing touch to the tea by providing a pop of flavor. I like to grow accent ingredients in my garden. Lemon verbena makes a beautiful accent, as do calendula and strawberries. If the plant doesn't grow in your climate, consider buying the herbs at the store. Measure one part of the accent ingredient.

Lastly, combine the three ingredients in a bowl. Measure out two teaspoons to one tablespoon and brew your delicious cup of artisanal herbal tea.

Medicinal Blends

Herbs aren't just for tea. They may be used for cooking, infused in oil to make body care products, macerated with salts or sugars for a bath, or dried and added to sachets for potpourri.

Herbs are rich in essential oils and provide many therapeutic and medicinal benefits. The essential oils in herbs can help relieve a headache, soothe an upset stomach, clear a stuffy nose, or support you during a cold. Making your own herbal tea blends means you are in control of what you add, and if you have grown the herbs yourself, you know the ingredients are organic and sustainable. There's no better feeling than having herbs at your fingertips when you need them.

I love heading to the garden when I need a bunch of one herb or another. The aroma can be intoxicating and uplifting, and I often stop and rub the leaves, releasing their incredible scent. If you plan your herb garden, it can provide wonderful tisanes and many medicinal benefits.

Some herbs are "considered" medicinal but are not medically proven treatments, so don't substitute what is written in this book for a doctor's recommendation. Be sure to check with your doctor before starting any herbal treatments. Pregnant or nursing women need to check with their doctor before consuming any herbs because some may have an adverse effect on the mom or baby.

To get you started preparing your own medicinal blends, be sure to check out page 112 for my Rest and Relax Tea recipe.

Brewing Methods

When I first started drinking teas, I only knew of one way to brew them. I thought all tea, whether black, green, white, or herbal, was boiled and steeped in the same way. I boiled water, popped a tea bag in my mug, poured water over the tea bag, and waited for it to steep. It seemed simple enough, but the teas didn't always taste right.

But ever since I started growing my own herbs, I discovered there is more than one way to brew tea. This section will talk about three different ways to brew herbal teas: decoctions, infusions, and cold brewing.

Decoctions

Decoctions are necessary when the plant material is dense and therefore requires a longer brewing time. Brewing an herb in a saucepan of boiling water allows the heat of the water to soften and break down the herbs. Cooking them for a longer time allows the flavors and medicinal compounds to be fully extracted.

Roots, bark, and seeds, such as licorice, cinnamon, dandelion root, and rosehips, are best cooked to achieve an extraction because their tissues tend to be dry and hard. A short steep is not enough time or consistent heat to penetrate the cell walls and plant material.

For a decoction, place the roots in a saucepan and cover them with water. Bring the water to a boil, then simmer for at least twenty minutes until the roots have softened. Some decoctions can take longer; it depends on the number of roots, volume of water, and dryness of the plant material.

Some decoctions are prepared to produce herbal medicine (for example, echinacea root). You may also choose to make a decoction to produce a very flavorful tea. Dried orange peel, cinnamon, apple, and cranberries result in a very flavorful decoction that can be enjoyed during the fall and winter seasons.

Infusions

The traditional approach to making tea is by way of an infusion. Water is boiled to a specific temperature, usually 203°F to 210°F, then poured over the herbs. Herbs are left to steep for at least four or five minutes, then strained into a cup. Other infusions may take longer, but these are usually for medicinal purposes.

Unlike decoctions that essentially cook the herbs, for infusions, water is brought to a boil, then turned off. As the herbs steep in the water, the water slowly cools and is absorbed into the cell walls of the plant material. Flavors are gently extracted because the heat level cools as it infuses. Infusions are best when steeping leaves, flowers, and fruit. The longer the steep, the more flavorful the extraction.

Some plants contain tannins. Boiling water releases the tannins and causes the brew to taste bitter. Lowering the heat to between 195°F and 200°F will prevent the flavor of the tea being ruined by the release of tannins. For a successful infusion in lower-temperature water, leave the brew to steep for five to fifteen minutes, then strain. Through trial and error and experience, you will learn which herbs you prefer for tisanes, along with their best steeping time.

Cold Brewing

Cold brewing is the process of extracting a brew in cold water. The process is similar to an infusion, except it takes much longer, from eight to twenty-four hours. Leaves take at least eight hours to process in a cold brew, whereas roots need about twenty-four hours. Cold brewing flowers, fruit, and seeds fall somewhere in between.

The ideal way to do a cold brew is to add two or three tablespoons of the tea blend to a large glass canning jar or pitcher, then fill it to the top with water. Close the lid or cover with a towel and place the jar in the refrigerator. It is best to chill the brew as it extracts to prevent spoilage. To make things easy, set up the cold brew before bed and leave it in the refrigerator overnight. By morning, it will be ready.

A cold brew is like an infusion in that the leaves are left to soak while they extract their flavors and medicinal properties. However, it is different in that it takes cold water much longer to penetrate the cells of the plant material. The leaves start out dry; then, they need to absorb water and rehydrate. Once they rehydrate, steeping will begin. Cold brewing produces a sweet and gentle tea.

The Modern Tea Garden

It has never been easier to grow your own tea garden. Many herbs will grow well in containers and pots, right on your back deck or balcony. Growing your own tea garden gives you the freedom to choose what you like, and many herbs have more than one purpose.

Growing your own herbs has numerous benefits over buying store-bought bags. Herbs are right at your fingertips and can therefore be harvested fresh. You control the soil and can grow your plants without using harmful chemicals if you desire. A tea garden is sustainable, allowing you to be self-sufficient.

Store-bought tea bags usually contain ingredients that have traveled a long distance, often from across the globe. The ingredients are not fresh and are usually just a collection of broken herb bits and dust, often taken from the lower portion of the plant, which is of inferior quality. If you remember, the best tisanes are made using the newest growth at the top of the plant. This growth is usually reserved for loose-leaf herbal tea, which means store-bought tea bags are filled with lower-quality product.

When you grow your own herbal tea garden, you can enjoy the many benefits of growing and caring for a garden. It is a relaxing and enjoyable experience that is both healthy and fulfilling.

CHAPTER 2

A Guide to Getting Your Hands Dirty

Now that you've learned about teas and tisanes, it's time to grow your own tea garden. In this chapter, I will cover all that is involved in doing just that, from choosing the ideal location, tools you'll need, selecting plants, and more.

Although growing in the ground may seem like a simple solution, it has more cons than pros for a novice gardener, so I will share three other options, and you can choose which method will work best for you. By the end of this chapter, you'll know how to grow and harvest different teas, and you'll have four tea garden compilations to give you a head start.

Hardiness Zones

The USDA Plant Hardiness Zone map (see References for the link, page 120) covers growing zones across the United States based on the average minimum winter temperature. This map is a useful tool because it allows you to choose perennial plants suited to your climate. If a plant requires warmer temperatures, then you can plan to either grow that plant as an annual or grow it in a pot and bring it indoors to overwinter.

The USDA Hardiness Map is divided into thirteen different zones, with another thirteen subzones. For example, zone 8a covers a minimum temperature of 10°F to 15°F, whereas zone 5b covers a minimum temperature of −15°F to −10°F. When planning your garden, it is important to begin with your hardiness zone.

The tea plant, *Camellia sinensis*, is hardy in zones 7 to 9. That means that the tea plant can't handle temperatures lower than 0°F to 5°F. If your winter temperature drops below 5°F, grow your tea plants in containers, then bring them indoors to overwinter. If you live in hardiness zone 10 or higher, it is better to grow your tea plants in a shady location to protect them from afternoon sun and heat. Be sure to water the plants consistently and provide partial shade.

Tea Garden Basics

In this section, we'll talk about everything you need to know to grow your own tea garden. Although every location is different, the foundation of knowledge is the same.

I will cover how to choose the best location for your tea garden, where to best situate your plants, the light requirements of the plants, and other environmental factors. I'll discuss the best soil choices for containers, raised beds, and indoor gardens, including how to identify healthy soil and signs to watch for when soil becomes unhealthy.

Watering is an important consideration. Often, incorrect watering is the main cause of a failed garden. I will share the signs that indicate overwatering and underwatering, as well as different water types. Pruning is also important to maintain healthy plants, encourage new growth, and help create plant vigor. Different pruning techniques will be discussed to help your tea plants grow.

Pests are abundant in any garden, and some are more attracted to tea and medicinal plants than others. I will share how to deal with pests organically, protect your crops from attack, and help deter pests. These five sections are the basis of a successful tea garden and will help you feel confident about growing your own.

Location

For a tea garden, choosing a location with full sun is very important. Full sun can be defined as having six to eight hours of direct afternoon sunlight.

Most herbs and plants grow better when the sun is not blocked by trees, buildings, or other obstacles. Also, the afternoon sun is much stronger than the morning sun. If your backyard, balcony, or deck receives sunlight in the morning, but it is in the shade noon, then you are growing in partial sun, which won't be enough to grow many plants, particularly fruiting crops. It is best to find a location that receives full sun for at least six hours in the afternoon and place your garden there. Some plants will grow in partial sunlight, but your plant selections will be limited.

A partially sunny location can be used to grow many herbs, such as cilantro, sage, and thyme, as well as several berries, for example, raspberries and currants. Other popular herbs will grow in a partially sunny location but won't have enough energy to produce large and abundant plants. You would need to consider planting several of each species to achieve a large enough harvest to meet your needs.

Soil

Soil requirements vary depending on the garden type you choose, for instance in the ground, in raised beds, or in pots and containers. Healthy soil has a loamy consistency that balances silt, sand, and clay. It holds enough water and provides good drainage for air to reach the plant's roots. If your soil is heavy and poorly draining, you have clay soil. Sandy soil is mostly sand; although filled with air pockets, it won't hold any water.

Raised beds may be filled with a triple mix of soil, consisting of topsoil, compost, and other organic materials. Each year, I amend my raised beds with compost, leaf mulch, or organic matter, which enriches the soil and creates a loamy consistency.

Containers and pots may be filled with organic potting soil. This is sold by the bag and contains peat moss, perlite, vermiculite, and compost. Many brands of potting soil are available at nurseries and garden centers.

If you choose to plant your garden directly in the ground and find that you have either clay or sandy soil, you can help amend it by adding organic matter such as compost, composted manure, and organic mulches every year. Over time, it will help fix the soil structure, but it will require careful watering and attention until that time.

Watering

Plants are made up of cells containing water. For plants to be healthy, they need to be supplied with a consistent moisture level. When plant cells dry up, they become damaged, thereby hindering the movement and uptake of nutrients from the soil. Conversely, when plants are overwatered, their roots are flooded, filling the cells with water and causing them to break down. The flow of nutrients from the soil to the plant is impeded, further damaging plant health.

When watering plants, there are several options to choose from. Rainwater is the ideal source because it is free of chemicals, salts, minerals, and pharmaceuticals and is slightly acidic. Rainwater also contains nitrates, one of the macronutrients (N-P-K) necessary for plant growth. Have you ever noticed how lush and green the garden looks after a good rain? If you can, collect rainwater in a rain barrel and use it to keep your plants consistently watered.

Filtered well water is also suitable for plants. Avoid watering with fluoridated tap water because it is heavy in metals, minerals, and chemicals. If your plants are growing in small pots indoors, choose distilled water. The most common sign of both overwatering or underwatering is the yellowing of leaves, which unfortunately often leads to further overwatering.

Pruning

Pruning plants is beneficial to stimulate new growth, create a bushier form, prevent plants from going to seed, remove old or sick growth, and prevent pests.

There are several ways to prune herb plants. Pinching back the top growth at the leaf joint is an excellent way to prevent your plants from going to seed or bolting. For example, basil, rosemary, anise hyssop, and mint tend to form a flower cluster at the growth tip when plants start bolting. To prevent this and extend the life of your plants, cut back at the joint where the leaf meets the main stem, and your plants will then branch out, creating a bushier plant.

If your plants don't have a leaf joint (for example, chamomile, calendula, lemongrass, and red clover), then either remove the flowers to encourage more flower production or cut back the entire stem. A final way to prune is to cut the whole plant back by one-third to one-half. Don't prune back further than this, or you will stunt the plant's growth. It is best to do this after the growing season at harvest time or in midsummer, so the plants still have time to produce another flush of growth.

Pests

The tea plant attracts several insect pests. Spider mites are tiny, eight-legged insects that, unsurprisingly, resemble spiders. They are typically found on the undersides of leaves, where they form a very fine weblike covering. If left unattended, leaves will develop a mottled appearance, eventually turning yellow and preventing new growth.

Over fifty types of scale insect may affect *Camellia sinensis*, with tea scale being the most common. Scale insects are often found on the underside of leaves, where they leave a sticky, honeylike covering. A common pest you might see is aphids, which look like tiny flies with or without wings; these vary in color from brown to black, red, or yellow. Aphids gather in tight groups and feed on flowers, stems, and leaves. They often attract ants, and they leave behind sooty mold.

To deal with pests, I recommend pruning back your plants by one-third and spraying with insecticidal soap (dish soap diluted with water) or using a horticultural oil such as neem. Alternatively, spray the pests with a strong stream of water, which will help dislodge them.

Medicinal plants contain essential oils and chemical compounds that naturally deter pests. Planting medicinal plants next to other plants in your garden will help keep your plants pest-free.

Essential Gardening Tools

A garden cannot be worked without certain garden tools. These tools are necessary to fulfill all the tasks of weeding, planting, maintaining, and harvesting. Although many more tools than those listed here are available, you don't need them to achieve a successful harvest. These five garden tools are enough to get you started growing your own tea garden.

Garden gloves: Soil contains many microbes. Although good for plants, they are not very good for your hands. Gloves protect your skin from cuts, bug bites, and potential infections. They also help keep your hands clean.

Hand fork: A small hand fork helps dig out stubborn weeds, lift roots, loosen compacted soil, and spread organic mulch.

Hand pruner or garden scissors: Depending on the sturdiness of the plant and thickness of its stems, you will need either pruners or scissors for harvesting and pruning.

Hand trowel: A small hand shovel, the trowel digs holes and makes transplanting seedlings a breeze. It is also helpful for scooping compost and organic fertilizer into planting holes.

Watering can or watering wand: No matter where you are growing your plants, a watering can or watering wand is necessary for watering your garden.

Choosing a Garden That Grows with You

Creating a new garden is exciting! You have many options to choose from, depending on what you dream of getting from your garden. For a new gardener, growing in a raised bed is simple. Kits are available that are click and go. You may choose to build a raised bed yourself. If space is limited, a container garden on a deck or balcony can consist of pots, grow bags, or a raised garden planter. Growing indoors is also a possibility if you don't have access to outdoor space.

Although an in-ground garden may seem like an easy option, it isn't a simple matter of just digging a hole and planting in the ground. There are several factors to consider. For starters, your soil may be a challenge. Soil is rarely loamy and ready to be planted; rather, it may be rocky, sandy, or possibly clay. If there is a lawn, this needs to be taken up first, along with all the weeds. The time and physical labor spent preparing the garden will delay planting and harvest.

Is the pH of your soil acidic or alkaline? Neither extreme is conducive for growing all plants, herbs, and vegetables. The ideal pH should be slightly acidic, from 5.8 to 6.5. Anything outside that range will affect plant vigor and nutrition. You can easily find soil testing kits to help you assess your soil.

Heavy rains, wind exposure, and drying sun are challenges to an in-ground garden. When growing in the ground, the plants are exposed to all weather conditions without true protection. At ground level, the garden is easily accessible by wildlife that will likely view your plants as an attractive buffet. Soilborne pests such as pill bugs, slugs, and snails may also present a challenge.

Container and Indoor Gardening

Growing in a container garden means placing your pots where you want them, such as on a deck or balcony. There are many inexpensive container options to choose from. Your garden could be as simple as a few pots of various sizes or as large as a planting container on legs.

The pros of growing in a container garden include control over light, soil, and watering. If the weather suddenly cools or a heavy storm is forecast, it is easy to slip your pots indoors for protection. Many crops are better suited for containers; for example, mint has aggressive roots spread by rhizomes and, if grown in an in-ground garden, is difficult to control. Blueberries are another great choice for containers because they require acidic soil, which may be purchased easily.

Although a container garden has many pros, there are a few cons to consider before you decide. As a plant grows, its roots grow with it. In a container, that space may quickly be used up, causing the plant to become rootbound. Watering needs to be more frequent and consistent because the small volume of soil in containers heats up and dries quickly. Forgetting to water will cause the plants to dry.

WATERING

To properly water a container garden, allow the water to evenly penetrate the soil and come out through the drainage holes. It is best to water your container garden in the morning or late afternoon, although midday watering is acceptable if the plants have begun to wilt. Avoid watering at night or in the evening because doing so will attract pests to the wet soil and foliage.

The pros of watering containers are several. For example, you know when your pots are sufficiently watered, and you have control over how much water each pot receives. To gauge if they are sufficiently watered, lift or tilt each pot. If it feels light, it needs more water. If it feels heavy, it is sufficiently watered.

Although there are many pros to watering a container, it is difficult to ignore the cons. Because containers sit above the ground, the soil inside them heats up quickly on a hot and sunny day. If the pot is made of black plastic, it will heat faster and dry faster. Be sure to water your containers at least twice a day on hot, sunny days and at least once a day the rest of the time, unless heavy rains are forecast.

DRAINAGE

When selecting containers, be sure to choose those with good drainage holes. Proper drainage is very important to ensure water won't pool inside the pots. If water does sit inside the pots, it will close the air pockets within the soil and choke the plant roots. Excess water also leads to powdery mildew, mold, and plant and root rot. It is very difficult to manage moisture levels without drainage holes, especially when growing outside, because rain will constantly flood containers.

If your only option is a container without drainage holes, there are two things you can do. The first is to drill holes with the proper drill bit. Three to five drainage holes are all you need. The second is to plant your herbs in a plastic pot and use that as an insert for the decorative outer container. When watering, pull the plastic pot out from the exterior container and water your plants. After the excess water has drained, return the plastic pots to their decorative outer containers.

Grow bags, raised planter gardens, railing planters, and container gardens will have appropriate drainage holes, making their use easy and worry-free. Stand the containers on plant saucers. This will help with drainage and protect the surface under the container.

SOIL

Because garden soil is too heavy to use in containers or pots, begin with potting soil. There are many varieties sold by the bag at nurseries and garden centers. I like to amend my potting soil with perlite and vermiculite, creating lighter soil and improving moisture retention. Worm castings and a well-balanced fertilizer will help feed your plants.

To amend the container, fill two-thirds of it with potting soil. Fill the remaining one-third with equal parts perlite and vermiculite, a few handfuls of worm castings, and a couple tablespoons of well-balanced fertilizer. Stir the mixture together by hand or using a hand trowel.

PRUNING AND REPOTTING

It is important to stay on top of pruning to prevent plants from becoming long and leggy, then flowering and setting seed. Pinch back branching herbs, such as mint, basil, anise hyssop, and other mint family plants, just above where the main stem meets a leaf joint. This will encourage the plant to branch out, which will create a bushier habit.

For plants that don't branch out but instead develop new stems at the base, harvest individual stems from the outside in. All other herbs may be cut back by one-third to produce new growth and develop a better form. Flowering herbs can be pruned by removing flower stems or snipping off individual flowers.

Keep an eye on plants that may benefit from repotting. When plant roots start emerging from drainage holes, your plant is ready for a larger pot. Plants that have been in the same soil for several years and are starting to show signs of decline would benefit from being repotted with fresh soil because old soil can become inert. Pull plants up from the container. If the roots are tightly bound, also known as root-bound, the plants are ready for repotting in a larger container.

SUNLIGHT

Be sure to place your container garden in a sheltered, sunny location. This will prevent wind from blowing your pots over and can often result in a mini microclimate garden. Heat trapped in the wall from the afternoon sun raises the temperature around the plants, potentially improving on the rest of your area's hardiness zone and allowing you to grow plants that wouldn't otherwise be capable of growing in your area.

Should the sun disappear or shift by midday, growing in a container allows you to move your plants to follow the sun. If a downpour or early frost is forecast, moving containers under a roof or into a garage will protect them and extend the growing season.

Raised-Bed Gardening

If you would like to grow many herbs and vegetables, a raised bed is a good choice. I love growing in my raised-bed kitchen garden. The taller beds are easier to work with, keeping me from bending and also allowing me to sit on the sides.

There are many pros to growing in a raised-bed garden. Soil is a major advantage because you can choose the best soil, then improve it with yearly organic amendments. Raised beds require less watering than containers do, because the soil doesn't dry out as quickly.

When choosing a location for your garden, you have the freedom of selecting the sunniest spot for the raised bed. In the spring, raised beds will warm up faster than garden soil, allowing you to plant earlier. Unlike containers, raised beds can be built to be as large and long as you like. Beds built to be at least two feet tall will help keep cottontail rabbits out.

There are only a few cons to growing in a raised bed. One is that once placed, you can't move them. The cost of lumber is higher than containers and pots, and a raised bed requires a lot more soil to get started.

WATERING

There are many options for watering a raised bed. Drip irrigation is a system whereby a series of thin hoses with small holes are evenly spaced throughout the bed and exude water one drop at a time on a set timer. This is the easiest method because it requires little work once set up, but it prevents you from noticing any plant problems when they occur.

A watering wand and hose take time but allow you to observe your plants and notice any problems as they occur. If pests or diseases are present, they can be dealt with immediately. Although using a watering can is a simple approach, it requires more refills and effort to water deeply and thoroughly.

SOIL

A simple solution for filling raised beds is with triple mix. Triple mix is sold by the yard; have it delivered, then use a wheelbarrow to move and dump it into each raised bed. A two-inch-thick layer of garden compost or composted manure can be spread over the soil's surface. Use a rake to smooth it out and break up large lumps. It is not necessary to turn the compost in; just let it settle for a couple of days, then plant directly into the soil. Over time, worms will move the compost from the surface down into the depths of the raised-bed garden.

PRUNING

Pruning in a raised bed is different from pruning in a container garden because a raised bed is permanent, and the plants can expand their roots and grow large. Depending on the plant you are growing, an herb may be pruned throughout the growing season by pinching back growing tips and harvesting entire stems and branches. At the end of the growing season, a perennial herb may be cut back by one-third to one-half, leaving the rest of the plant to go dormant for the winter. This practice applies to herbs such as sage, thyme, lavender, and rosemary.

Perennial plants such as black currant, raspberry, and blueberry may be pruned in late winter. Cut back diseased and damaged wood, as well as any old stems that no longer produce fruit. It is best to prune at this time of year, because once plant growth begins in the spring, any exposed cuts will become targets for pests and diseases. Use the empty spaces around perennial plants to grow annual herbs until the perennial plants outgrow the empty space.

Herbs such as lemongrass, turmeric, and ginger are harvested entirely at the end of the growing season and do not require pruning. Leave them to grow until harvest time.

PESTS

Raised beds are exposed to all plant pests. In a garden, slugs, snails, earwigs, and ants will crawl into the beds and lay their eggs under the soil. They aren't a terrible nuisance, but a wet and rainy summer may increase their numbers and make them a problem. Depending on the growing conditions, aphids may be present. Herbs tend to attract fewer pests than other plants in the garden due to their aromatics and high essential oil content. Herbs may act as companion plants for vegetables and help prevent and deter pests.

STARTING SEEDS INDOORS AND TRANSPLANTING

If you choose to start seeds indoors, purchase fresh seeds and be sure to read the growing information on the seed packet. Begin with a good seed-starting mix and amend it with worm castings and a little vermiculite. This mixture will give the seedlings some beneficial nutrients, help lighten the soil, and add moisture-retaining properties.

Mix well, moisten, and fill your selected seed trays. I prefer to sow two or three seeds per cell to guarantee at least one will germinate. Plant the seeds at a depth of three times the size of the seed, cover with the clear plastic humidity dome, and set the seed trays under grow lights. If you don't have grow lights, select your sunniest west-facing window, and place the trays directly in front of it.

Once the seeds germinate, remove the plastic dome and water when the soil is partially dry. When the seedlings develop their first true leaves, or at least four sets of leaves in total, transplant the seedlings into four-inch pots.

Two weeks before the final frost date (the dates for your zip code can be found online easily), start hardening off the seedlings by bringing them outdoors into a sheltered spot for a short while during the day and increasing the length of time daily until the plants are outside full time. Transplant the seedlings into the garden beds or containers when they have been fully hardened off.

SUNLIGHT

Because raised beds cannot be moved once built and filled, it is important that you choose the best location for your garden. Start by watching where the sun moves throughout the day. Take note of the hours of sun as it moves through your garden and remember that morning sun is gentler than afternoon sun. Select a spot that is open and away from trees, walls, or neighboring fences. Ideally, you should place your garden where it will receive a minimum of six to eight hours of full afternoon sun. Anywhere else and plant growth and final harvest will be negatively affected.

PICKING PLANTS FOR YOUR ZONE

A raised-bed garden will grow perennial and annual plants unlike containers and pots that may be moved inside and grown as houseplants. When selecting perennial plants for your beds, be sure to select suitable ones for your hardiness zone (see page 18).

Camellia sinensis is hardy in zones 7 to 9. If you live outside these zones, it is better to grow the plant in a container, then move it indoors. For other perennial plants and herbs, check the hardiness zone of each one and only select plants that will have no trouble overwintering in your garden.

Indoor Gardening

I have attempted to grow tea plants indoors. I always wanted to grow one and searched far and wide to find one. I ended up finding two, but to grow them outside was impossible. My hardiness zone is much too cold for the *Camellia sinensis* plant, so I grew them as houseplants indoors.

If you don't have a backyard, deck, or balcony, it is possible to grow your own tea and herb plants indoors. It won't be as simple as growing the plants outside, but by following several steps, you will be able to get a harvest.

To be successful, pay attention to the amount of light the plant will receive because, without it, your plants won't grow, will grow lanky, or may be susceptible to pests. Watering is also very important because too much or not enough water will contribute to other problems.

In this section, I will discuss proper indoor watering techniques for your plants, the differences between sunlight and grow lights, pruning and repotting techniques, healthy soil, and the possible pests that may impact your tea and herb plants.

WATERING

Thorough, deep watering will result in healthier indoor plants than light watering. Plant your tea and herb plants in plastic nursery pots with drainage holes to ensure proper drainage. Water the plants when they feel almost dry, and always water them from below. To do this, fill the sink with several inches of water, then lift the pots and set them in the sink to absorb water until the soil is fully saturated. If a plant is too large to lift, water from above with a watering can and wait until the water has been evenly absorbed.

SUNLIGHT

If you have a bright south- or west-facing window, place the plants as close to the window as possible. The farther your plants sit from the window, the fewer foot candles of light they will receive. (A foot candle is a measurement of light intensity on one square foot of surface with a uniform light source.) Bear in mind that the side of the plant facing into the room receives much less light, explaining why plants seem to lean into the window as they grow. Actually, they are growing longer on the window side. If you are growing in the light from a window, turn the plant daily to create a more even overall growth.

In the northern hemisphere, the winter sun sits low and supplies very few foot candles of light through the window. If you live in the north, consider purchasing a grow light for your plants. This can be a track of fluorescent or LED lights or a simple LED lamp. Many options are available on the market. Plants need at least sixteen hours of sunlight to grow indoors successfully. Set the light timer to run sixteen hours on and eight hours off to simulate full sun.

PRUNING

Every plant benefits from a good pruning, including *Camellia sinensis*. During the winter, the tea plant is dormant. In the spring, new leaves start to grow, and the plant is ready for harvest. By harvesting, you are essentially pruning the plant. Pluck the top few leaves and remove any dead or dying leaves. In the winter, clean up any dead growth. For established plants, prune the plant back by one-half to keep the size under control because plants can grow to six feet.

Here's how to tell when a plant is ready for repotting. Take a look at the roots. If they are emerging through the drainage holes or the plant is growing poorly, it has probably outgrown its pot. Carefully pull out the plant and observe. If the roots are root-bound, they will be wound tightly with little soil between them. Gently tease the roots apart or trim them back. Then repot the plant into a larger pot. To repot, fill the pot with moistened organic potting mix and add a handful of worm castings. Mix well to ensure even distribution of the castings. Place the plant into the pot and press down to firm the soil, setting the plant in evenly. Top with extra topsoil, if needed. Repot every two to four years.

SOIL

The appropriate potting mix for containers and houseplants is essential. *Camellia sinensis* prefers acidic potting soil rather than regular potting soil. If you have trouble sourcing acidic soil, regular potting soil can be amended with sulfur or evergreen needles to help lower the pH level.

Do not allow your tea plants to have wet roots. Soggy soil will lead to root rot. Be sure to select a well-draining soil and allow the plant to drain completely before setting it back.

Consider amending the soil with an organic fertilizer. Worm castings, also known as worm manure, are a gentle and excellent fertilizer. Sprinkle a thin layer on the soil surface, then scratch it into the soil. Over time the soil will be enriched, resulting in a loamier texture with improved soil structure. Other amendment options include fish emulsion (an organic by-product of the fishing industry) or compost tea. Compost tea may be made with worm castings and is available in prepared tea bags.

Over time, soil becomes inert and lifeless as the plants take up nutrients. When you notice that the plants have stopped growing, it is time to repot. Repot and change the potting soil no more than once a year and only in the spring.

PESTS

When indoor conditions are not ideal and soil moisture is constant, the tea plant becomes vulnerable to pest attack. Common pests of *Camellia sinensis* include aphids, scale insect, and spider mites. All these pests cause a reduction in tea plant growth and harvest.

Aphids will attack new growth on the growing tips of the tea plant. Although aphids may be washed or sprayed off with water, they injure the plants by sucking plant juices out of the leaves.

There are many varieties of scale insects that will attack tea plants. Scale insects sit on the underside of leaves. The damage they cause affects plant growth, with new leaves often falling off. If undetected, scale can kill part of or the entire plant.

Spider mites may be found all over the plant but can be hard to detect unless they produce a fine weblike netting. Leaves will become discolored and lifeless. Any damage from pests will affect new plant growth and harvest. To prevent pests, use a humidifier over the winter and lower indoor temperature.

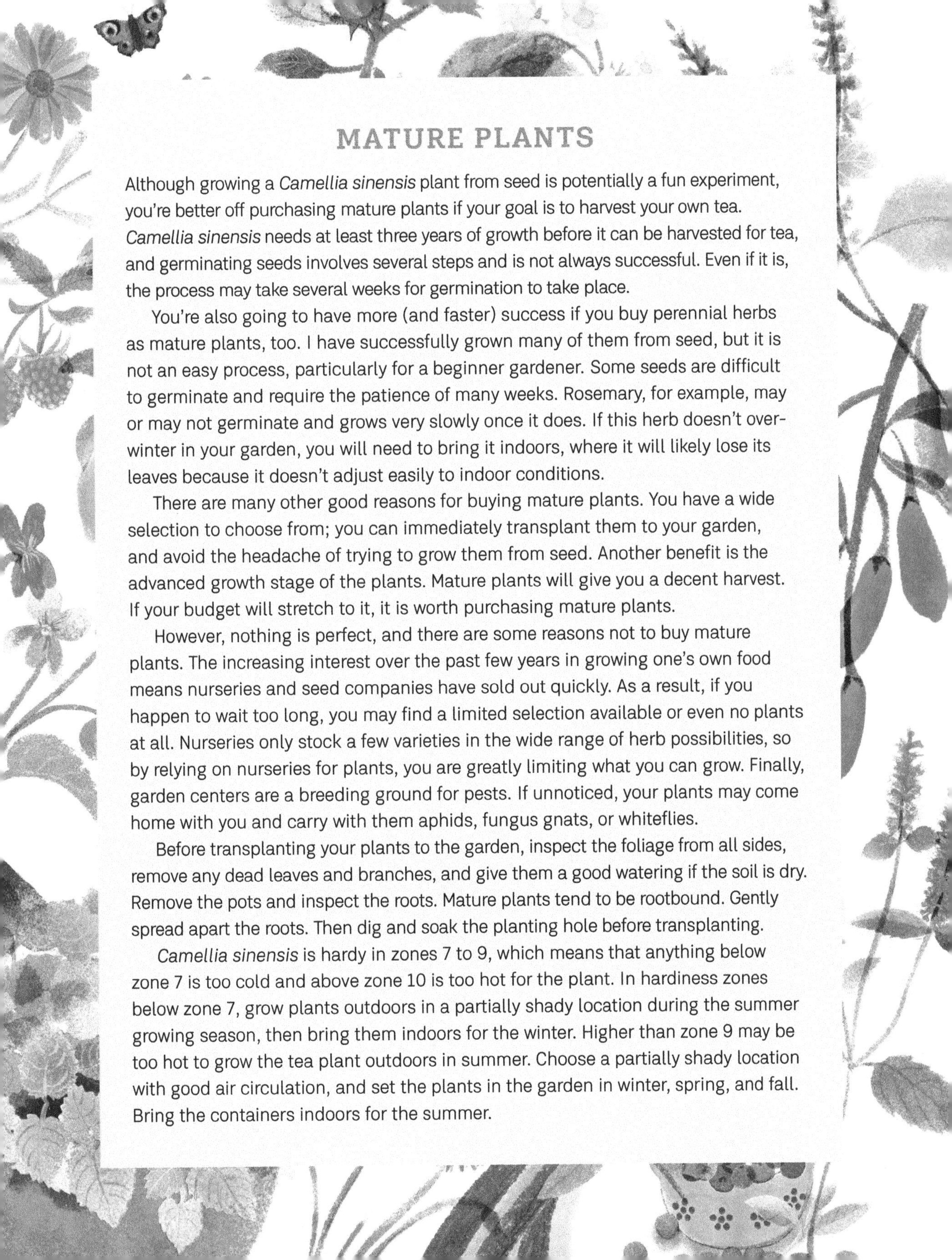

MATURE PLANTS

Although growing a *Camellia sinensis* plant from seed is potentially a fun experiment, you're better off purchasing mature plants if your goal is to harvest your own tea. *Camellia sinensis* needs at least three years of growth before it can be harvested for tea, and germinating seeds involves several steps and is not always successful. Even if it is, the process may take several weeks for germination to take place.

You're also going to have more (and faster) success if you buy perennial herbs as mature plants, too. I have successfully grown many of them from seed, but it is not an easy process, particularly for a beginner gardener. Some seeds are difficult to germinate and require the patience of many weeks. Rosemary, for example, may or may not germinate and grows very slowly once it does. If this herb doesn't overwinter in your garden, you will need to bring it indoors, where it will likely lose its leaves because it doesn't adjust easily to indoor conditions.

There are many other good reasons for buying mature plants. You have a wide selection to choose from; you can immediately transplant them to your garden, and avoid the headache of trying to grow them from seed. Another benefit is the advanced growth stage of the plants. Mature plants will give you a decent harvest. If your budget will stretch to it, it is worth purchasing mature plants.

However, nothing is perfect, and there are some reasons not to buy mature plants. The increasing interest over the past few years in growing one's own food means nurseries and seed companies have sold out quickly. As a result, if you happen to wait too long, you may find a limited selection available or even no plants at all. Nurseries only stock a few varieties in the wide range of herb possibilities, so by relying on nurseries for plants, you are greatly limiting what you can grow. Finally, garden centers are a breeding ground for pests. If unnoticed, your plants may come home with you and carry with them aphids, fungus gnats, or whiteflies.

Before transplanting your plants to the garden, inspect the foliage from all sides, remove any dead leaves and branches, and give them a good watering if the soil is dry. Remove the pots and inspect the roots. Mature plants tend to be rootbound. Gently spread apart the roots. Then dig and soak the planting hole before transplanting.

Camellia sinensis is hardy in zones 7 to 9, which means that anything below zone 7 is too cold and above zone 10 is too hot for the plant. In hardiness zones below zone 7, grow plants outdoors in a partially shady location during the summer growing season, then bring them indoors for the winter. Higher than zone 9 may be too hot to grow the tea plant outdoors in summer. Choose a partially shady location with good air circulation, and set the plants in the garden in winter, spring, and fall. Bring the containers indoors for the summer.

Planning Your Plants

An annual plant completes its entire life cycle in one growing season. Seeds are planted; the plant grows and matures, flowers, and produces seeds; and the life cycle is complete.

On the other hand, a perennial plant grows, flowers, and sets seed each year, but the root system doesn't expire. Some plants will die back to the ground, and others will only lose their leaves but maintain their structure. In the spring, the plant grows anew and either produces all-new growth or leafs out and increases from its previous size. When you plant a perennial plant in your garden, you need to account for it being there over the long term, filling the space as its roots expand.

Annual plants are planted each year. Depending on the length of the plant's life cycle, a succession planting may be required, which means that as one plant comes to the end of its life cycle, another plant is planted. To extend the life of annual plants, it is best to harvest regularly to prevent the plant from flowering and setting seed.

Perennial plants may be planted in the spring, but they also thrive when planted in the fall. Because they are hardy in your growing zone, they will survive the winter and establish their roots before producing new growth the following year.

Harvesting Tea

Unlike pruning (see page 29), herbs may be harvested as often as you need throughout the growing season. Only harvest what you need each time, as taking too much may slow plant growth. At the end of the season, a more complete harvest may occur, where you cut annual herbs down to the ground because they are only viable for one growing season. Perennial herbs may be pinched as needed, or entire stems may be harvested, depending on how much you need. Perennial herbs may be cut back by half for a final season's harvest.

Only pinch back the new growth when harvesting from the tea plant, leaving older leaves and stems on the plant. In early spring, harvest the closed leaf bud for white tea and possibly an additional top leaf. To harvest for green tea, harvest the top two just-opened leaves and the bud because you want the youngest leaves for this tea. Later in the spring or summer, harvest the more mature top two leaves and leaf bud for black tea. For a harvest of oolong tea, harvest the top three leaves and leaf bud. More mature leaves will make a darker oolong, whereas younger leaves will produce a lighter oolong.

Essential Tools

Harvesting herbs can be a time-consuming task, as you process each stem, then strip off each leaf or flower. Chamomile, for example, can take over an hour to carefully pick each flower by hand, then gently place it in your harvest basket. This task can be done with your bare hands, or you can use tools to speed up the job.

Here are five essential tools to help you harvest and preserve your herbs and tea leaves to simplify the work.

Basket: A wicker basket made of natural plant materials is airy and breathable, making it ideal for herb and flower collection.

Dehydrator: A dehydrator is a quick solution for drying your herbs. Temperature is controllable to dry herbs evenly without the risk of scorching.

Garden snips or scissors: Garden snips are lightweight and have a good spring, saving your hand from aches and tension pain. Use snips to snip off flowers, leaves, and entire stems carefully.

Gardening gloves: Herb plants may have thorns, sharp edges, and insects. A good pair of gardening gloves will protect your hands while you harvest.

Herb stripper: This is a stainless-steel tool with six different-size holes. Pull stems through the appropriate size hole and easily separate leaves from the stem.

These five tools are all you really need for harvest and preservation. One tool may be swapped out for a different one, and there are certainly more to choose from. If you don't have a dehydrator, you can tie your herbs in bundles and hang them upside down to dry. Wire racks may also be used for drying in a dark, ventilated space.

HARVEST LIKE A PRO

Two common harvesting mistakes are cutting back too much of the plant, thereby stunting growth, and harvesting at the wrong time of day. To harvest like a pro, choose early morning, just as the dew has dried off plant leaves and the essential oil content is high. Don't harvest from immature plants because this will affect the production of new leaves. Trim back to no more than the second set of leaves, leaving at least half a stem. This cut will encourage the development of side branching at the point where the stem meets leaves, creating a bushier plant. Be sure to use a clean knife or garden snips, wiping the blades with alcohol before moving on to the next plant.

If harvesting for leaves, be sure to do so before the plant begins producing flowers. If harvesting for flowers, it is better to snip them off before they are fully open. Mature flowers contain seeds and lack aroma and flavor. When harvesting seeds for tea (for example, coriander and fennel seeds), do so after they just turn brown and begin drying. Roots are best harvested in the fall after the plant foliage has died back. Ginger and turmeric roots are ready for harvest when the plant leaves have browned.

Turning Your Harvest into Tea

There are several techniques for properly drying tea. The plant material may be laid out on racks and placed in a dehydrator. Set the temperature between 95°F and 110°F and dehydrate until the leaves and leaf veins are crispy dry. To test for moisture, bend the leaf vein. If it's pliable, dehydrate for another six hours and test again. Air-drying is another option. Dry tea on racks in a dark room with good air circulation until the leaves are crispy dry. You may also tie them into bundles and hang them upside down.

Store loose-leaf teas and herbs in an airtight container. Glass containers are best, as any leftover moisture in the plant material will show up as moisture on the walls of the jar. Plastic containers tend to hold moisture better than glass. Plastic zip-top bags with ventilation holes may also be used, and they take up less space than jars.

Herbs will store well for at least one year, and teas may store for two or more years, depending on the type of tea. Test for freshness by smelling the tea. If the tea has an aroma, it is fresh. Stale and old tea leaves will have no scent and may be added to the compost pile.

Green Tea

For the best green tea, harvest in the spring while the leaves are young and fresh. Use your hands to pluck off the top two freshly opened leaves and the bud. As soon as the leaves are picked, it is important to stop oxidation. Either lay the leaves out on a bamboo rack for one or two hours to wither or steam them for one or two minutes. After steaming, run cold water over the leaves to stop the heat and protect their bright green color.

Before drying, the leaves need to be rolled. Place them in your hands and roll them into your preferred shape, either long tubes or little balls. The leaves will be tender and easy to work with.

After rolling for several minutes, dry the leaves in the oven at a low temperature of 212°F to 230°F. Spread the leaves out on a baking sheet, and after five minutes, gently turn the leaves over to ensure even drying. Any leftover moisture will have evaporated at this point, and the leaves will be fully dry. Loose-leaf green tea is best stored in an airtight glass jar in a dark cupboard.

White Tea

White tea has a very short harvest window, usually only for two weeks in the spring. Keep an eye on your plants and harvest the white downy buds while the leaves are drawn together or just as they begin to open. After harvest, the buds need immediate withering for several hours in a warm, well-ventilated location. This will help them release some of their moisture.

Unlike green tea, white tea is minimally processed and is not rolled. To prevent any oxidation after withering, lay the tea leaves out on racks to dry. This can be done in a well-ventilated, shaded location or at a very low temperature in the dehydrator. As the tea leaves dry, check on them and gently move them around, ensuring that all parts of the leaves are drying evenly. Once they are fully dry and brittle, store the white tea in an airtight glass container away from direct sunlight.

Black Tea

Harvest black tea later in the season, because the more mature leaves are chosen for this tea. Harvest the leaf bud and top two leaves and lay them out on a rack or mesh screen to wither for at least twenty-four hours. This will allow the leaves to lose about 60 percent of their moisture. After the leaves have been softened through withering, they are ready to be rolled. Using your hands, roll the leaves into tubes; by doing so, you will be releasing the enzymes in the cell walls, triggering oxidation. By the time you are finished, the tea leaves will be brown.

Once rolling is complete, the tea leaves are ready for drying. Lay them out on a baking sheet and dry at a low oven temperature of 240°F for twenty minutes. By the time the leaves are fully dry they will be crispy and ready for storage. Tea is best stored in an airtight container such as a glass jar. Store out of direct sunlight, preferably in a dark cupboard or pantry.

Oolong Tea

Harvest the top three leaves and the leaf bud to make oolong tea. These tea leaves are harvested later in the season to pick larger, more mature leaves. After harvest, tea leaves need to be withered to release excess moisture. In a well-ventilated room, lay the leaves out on mesh screens or racks for at least two hours. Creating your own unique oolong tea is a craft, and this is accomplished through oxidation. The less time you oxidize the leaves, the lighter the flavor; the longer the leaves oxidize, the stronger the resulting taste. For oxidation to occur, leaves need to remain on the screens while they are stirred periodically over a period of twelve to eighteen hours. You can experiment with the length of oxidation until you find your desired taste preference.

Once oxidation is complete, the leaves require rolling. This step will break down cell walls and release enzymes, darkening the leaves. To finish the process, oolong leaves require drying. Set the oven to 240°F and let the leaves dry on baking sheets for up to twenty minutes. By the time the drying process is complete, the leaves will be crispy dry. Store in an airtight glass jar or container.

Leaves

Harvest herbs first thing in the morning, because this is when the essential oil content is highest. Using garden snips, cut back each stem by one-third or up to the second leaf joint. For non-branching stems, cut back entire leaves at their base, working from the outside in. If the leaves need a rinse, do so quickly through a colander or by hand, then lay them between paper towels to absorb excess water.

Herbs may be dried in several ways. Tie the herb bundles together with kitchen string or twine and hang them upside down in a well-ventilated space, out of direct sunlight. Herbs may be laid out on racks or trays and left to dry, or they may be dried in a dehydrator at a very low temperature. This process can take anywhere from ten to twelve hours or longer if air dried. Once herbs are crispy dry, they are ready for the next step.

Separate the leaves from the stems, usually by rubbing them in the opposite direction, when they should fall off easily. At this point, they may be stored whole or broken into pieces. Store loose-leaf herbs in an airtight glass jar or container, preferably in a dark cupboard.

Flowers

The best time to harvest flowers is midmorning, just as the flower heads have begun to open and after the sun has dried any remaining dew off the petals. Late-day harvesting is okay, but the petals will have started closing and won't be as fresh. Using garden snips, cut at the base of the flower stems or directly under the flower head. Place harvested flowers in a basket, carefully laying them out without damaging them. I love calendula, and I find it best to harvest before midday when the flower petals begin to close and lose quality and medicinal value.

There are several ways to dry flowers. My favorite method is in a dehydrator set at a low temperature between 95°F and 100°F. Spread the flowers out on the racks without touching and check on them every hour until they are fully dry. Alternatively, lay out the flowers on a tray or tie them into bundles and dry them upside-down out of direct sunlight. Store the flowers in airtight glass jars or containers away from sunlight because exposure to air will fade them and cause their delicious aroma to evaporate.

Fruits

Fruits are best harvested when fully ripe and have reached their desired color. Unripe fruit will be a shade of green. You also want the fruit to smell and taste sweet and be at its optimal readiness at harvest. Harvest in the early morning, before the sun has had a chance to warm the fruit, because this is when it is sweetest. Give the fruit a taste; if the flavor is ideal, the fruit is ready.

Pick fruits or berries by hand and place them in a basket until you are ready to go indoors. Before drying, thoroughly inspect the fruit for any damage or worm holes. Wash and pat dry blemish-free fruit, then use a dehydrator for drying. Small berries such as elderberries, currants, and blueberries may be dried whole, whereas strawberries, pineapple, and other large fruit should be cut into slices or chunks before being laid out on dehydrator trays. Set the dehydrator at 125°F and turn it on. Fruit with higher water content such as strawberries will take longer to dry, whereas smaller fruit such as elderberries will take less time. Fruits are ready when squishing between two fingers doesn't leave any moisture on your skin, yet the fruit is pliable. Store in airtight glass jars.

Roots

Roots are best harvested in the fall, after a light frost. Although they may be harvested earlier, a frost or two will help sweeten them. At that time of year, the soil will be soft from frequent rains, and the roots should come up easily by hand. You may also use a garden fork or spade: Push the tool into the soil, several inches away from the base of the plant. Using the tool as a lever, gently lift the plant with its roots. Garden snips may be used to cut the roots into long pieces. If you want to regrow the plant, leave a few roots intact and replant them in the same location.

Bring the harvested roots into the kitchen and wash them well with a brush until all the soil has been removed. Chop the roots into thick slices and lay them on paper towels to absorb excess moisture. Roots may be dried in two different ways: a dehydrator for quick drying or out on a plate or tray for air-drying. Once the roots are fully dry and rock hard, store them whole in an airtight glass jar, or grind them into a powder before storage.

Preserving Tea

Before a tea may be stored, it must be fully dry. Once ready, teas are best preserved when kept out of direct sunlight and in an airtight container. A glass canning jar is a great option because the seal in the lid prevents air from getting into the jar. Keep the tea away from light, heat, and moisture, because these three factors will affect freshness and how long the tea will keep. Ideally, store jars of tea and herbs away from heating vents, cooking appliances, and water. On an open shelf in a dark kitchen cupboard or pantry is ideal.

Be sure to label your jars with the harvest date and specific tea ingredients: for example, "Tulsi basil, harvested July 2021." You may think you'll remember what all the jars contain, but you likely won't. If stored correctly, teas should last for at least one year and up to two years, depending on the tea. I have many that are over two years old. Although they are not as fresh as when newly harvested and dried, they are still aromatic and tasty. The best way to test for freshness is to smell the tea before brewing it. If the aroma is absent, the tea may be composted. If an aroma is present, the tea is good and can be brewed.

Specific Tea Gardens and Soil Mates

In this section, I have outlined four different garden compilation ideas to give you a head start in planning your first tea garden. Each compilation is designed to meet specific health and lifestyle needs, from digestive issues to getting a good sleep and stress relief to energizing morning brews to immune-boosting medicinal blends. For each compilation, I have listed the plants needed for the tea garden, the specific numbers of each plant, and the ideal garden type best suited to make it all work. Each garden corresponds with a tea blend recipe in chapter 7.

Tummy Tamer

To support digestive issues, plant a tea garden of mint, chamomile, basil, fennel, and ginger. All these herbs are very soothing to an upset stomach. Grow this garden in containers and pots, because several of the herbs will spread if left unchecked. You can find my Tummy Tamer Tea recipe on page 117.

Mint: 2 plants

Plant in a large pot to contain aggressive roots. The plants will spread and grow as tall as twelve inches (see page 54)

Chamomile: 1 plant

Although an annual, chamomile can drop seeds and self-sow. Harvest individual flowers before they open (see page 68).

Ginger: 1 or 2 roots

Ginger is a tropical herb but makes a beautiful houseplant. Plant in January in a large, deep, wide pot to allow the roots to spread and grow it outdoors during the summer. Bring the pot indoors and continue growing it over the winter (see page 104). Ginger will grow to a height of three or four feet.

Tulsi Basil: 3 plants

Plant in a large pot or separate pots. Pinch throughout the growing season (see page 58).

Fennel: 1 plant

Plant in a large pot and harvest the seeds before they drop. Fennel will grow to twenty-four inches.

Relaxation Mix

A garden that supports rest, relaxation, and sleep is one that contains beautiful plants. Chamomile, lavender, sweet violet, mint, and lemon balm are such plants. You can also add tulsi basil (see page 58) for its relaxing and medicinal properties. All these plants have properties that support a sense of calm and relaxation. Grow this garden in containers because mint and lemon balm can be invasive. Alternatively, this garden can be grown in raised beds, but reserve the invasive herbs for pots. See page 112 for my Rest and Relax Tea recipe.

Chamomile: 1 plant

Although an annual, chamomile can drop seeds and self-sow. Harvest individual flowers before they open (see page 68).

Lavender: 2 plants (see page 72)

Mint: 2 plants

Plant in a large pot to contain aggressive roots. The plants will spread and grow as tall as twelve inches (see page 54).

Lemon balm: 1 plant (see page 48)

Tulsi basil: 1 plant

This grows quite large and wide.

Sweet violets: As many as you like (see page 78)

These plants can be grown as a ground cover or foraged in chemical-free areas. They have anti-inflammatory properties and provide respiratory support. Sweet violets are perennial in zones 3 to 9 and are ready for harvest in the spring.

Energy Boost

Grab a mug and head outside to your morning brew garden. In this garden, you will find herbs that energize and help you get going. This compilation of plants is another potential container garden or raised-bed/container garden combination. However, I believe a container garden would be a better choice. See page 115 for my Energy Tea recipe.

Lemongrass: 1 plant (see page 52)

Lemon balm: 1 plant (see page 48)

Ginger: 2 roots

Ginger is a tropical herb but makes a beautiful houseplant. Plant in January in a large, deep, wide pot to allow the roots to spread, and grow it outdoors during the summer. Bring the pot indoors and continue growing it over the winter (see page 104). Ginger will grow to a height of three or four feet.

Turmeric: 2 roots (see page 108)

Plant in January in a large, wide, deep pot to allow the roots to spread. Turmeric will grow to a height of three or four feet.

Mint: 2 plants

Plant in a large pot to contain aggressive roots. The plants will spread and grow as tall as twelve inches (see page 54).

In a short growing season, hardiness zone 5 and lower, all containers can be brought indoors to grow by a sunny window. In hardiness zones 8 or higher, all containers can be left outside, with the exceptions of ginger and turmeric, because they are tropical plants.

Immune-Friendly Blends

If you would like to grow an herbal medicine cabinet, this garden combination will give you several herbs to strengthen your immune system and help combat the common cold. This garden should ideally be planted in raised beds, because several of the plants are perennial and require space for their roots to expand. For my Health and Wellness Tea recipe, see page 113.

Mint: 2 plants

Plant in a large pot to contain aggressive roots. The plants will spread and grow as tall as twelve inches (see page 54).

Anise: 1 plant (see page 46)

Calendula: 6 plants (see page 66)

Calendula will easily drop seed if flowers are left on the plant at the end of the season, so be prepared for volunteer plants. The more flowers you harvest, the more each plant will produce, allowing you to harvest regularly until the first frost.

Ginger: 2 roots

Ginger is a tropical herb but makes a beautiful houseplant. Plant in January in a large, deep, wide pot to allow the roots to spread and grow it outdoors during the summer. Bring the pot indoors and continue growing it over the winter (see page 104). Ginger will grow to a height of three or four feet.

Echinacea: 1 or 2 plants (see page 102)

Echinacea is perennial and requires at least three years for a harvest when grown from seed. For this reason, it is better to purchase mature plants.

Elderberry: 1 plant (see page 86)

Elderberry will grow into a large shrub yearly and may be cut back in late winter. It is harvested for its flowers and berries and is a powerful medicinal plant.

Licorice: 1 plant (see page 106)

PLANT TO TEA RATIO

When planning your garden and deciding on the number of plants you will need, first consider the types of teas you like to drink, the ingredients required for those tea blends, and how much and how often you drink them. Using this information, you will be able to work out the number of plants you'll need to sustain your tea-drinking habits.

Once you select your plants, consider the size of each plant, the quantity one plant will produce, and how quickly it regrows. For example, mint is a main ingredient of many herbal tea blends. This ingredient will require frequent harvesting, often harvesting large portions each time. After mint is dried, the volume will reduce significantly, and this needs to be accounted for in considering the number of plants required for the garden. So, if you plan on harvesting a lot of mint for tea, plant two to four mint plants.

Lavender has a pungent nature, and therefore only requires a small portion for tea blends. It grows slowly but drying won't shrink the flowers. In this case, you will require one or two lavender plants to attain a small to medium harvest.

CHAPTER 3

Leaves

ANISE

(Pimpinella anisum)

Common name(s): aniseed

PARTS USED: Seeds, leaves, and flowers

USES: Anise leaves and seeds can be used to make a delicious tea. Anise leaves can be tossed into salads to add flavor. The seeds are commonly used to flavor curries, cakes, pastries, cheeses, and breads, including German pfeffernuss, a special Christmas spice cookie. Anise oil is used to flavor drinks such as ouzo, absinthe, and sambuca.

Anise is commonly used to aid digestion and has antioxidant and antifungal properties. Crushed or ground seeds can be used in aromatic sachets. Anise seed oil can be used for making perfumes. Anise repels aphids as well as lice and other biting insects.

TASTE PROFILE: Strong licorice flavor

GROWING: Use seeds less than two years old. Sow anise seeds directly

in the garden or container where you plan to grow them, because they have a deep taproot that can be difficult to transplant. Anise grows equally well in outdoor containers, in raised beds, and in the ground. It can be grown indoors in the winter. If you're growing it in a container, make sure it is ten to twelve inches deep to accommodate the taproot. The plant will reach eighteen to thirty-six inches tall.

ANNUAL OR PERENNIAL: Annual

LIGHT: Full sun

WATERING: Anise does well in a somewhat dry environment. Let the soil dry out between waterings.

SOIL: Anise requires well-drained, light soil that is rich in organic material.

ZONE: Native to Egypt and the Mediterranean, anise prefers warmer temperatures but grows well in zones 4 to 11.

PRUNING: Generally, the plant doesn't require pruning.

COMPANIONS: Plant with cilantro to speed germination.

HARVESTING: Harvest the leaves as needed. Wait until the plants have flowered to harvest the seed heads.

SAFETY CONSIDERATIONS: Avoid using in large amounts when pregnant or breastfeeding. If you are allergic to asparagus, caraway, celery, coriander, cumin, dill, or fennel, you are also likely allergic to anise. May lower blood sugar levels.

PRESERVATION: Hang seed heads upside down in paper bags to dry. Store the seeds in glass jars in a cool, dark place for up to two years.

TIP: For anise seeds to germinate, the soil needs to be about 60°F.

LEMON BALM

(Melissa officinalis)

Common name(s): lemon balm

PARTS USED: Leaves and flowers

USES: Make hot or cold tea with the leaves. Add to cakes, cookies, jams, sorbet, and ice pops. Lemon balm simple syrup may be used to make cocktails.

Lemon balm is helpful for relieving bloating, gas, and indigestion. Contains vitamin C and is antibacterial and antiviral. Contains chemicals that may help you cope with stress, creating a calming effect and helping improve memory.

TASTE PROFILE: Flavor is best before the plant produces flowers. Strong lemon flavor, like lemon peel, but isn't sour. Leaves have a tough texture, making raw eating unappealing.

GROWING: Plants may be grown from seed or nursery-grown plant. Lemon balm could be grown in a container, in a raised bed, or in the ground. To prevent it from spreading, cut back before it self-seeds, plant in a container, or trim the edges to maintain form. It can reach up to two and a half feet tall. Divide plants in the spring or fall to increase supply.

ANNUAL OR PERENNIAL: Perennial

LIGHT: Full sun to partial shade

WATERING: Average watering requirements; the more you water the more actively it will grow.

SOIL: Grows in average, dry to medium, well-drained soils

ZONE: Hardy in zones 3 to 7

PRUNING: Cut back plants during the summer to remove spent flowers, prevent self-seeding, and encourage new growth.

COMPANIONS: Plant lemon balm with basil, fennel, rosemary, and sage. Lemon balm will grow with anything.

HARVESTING: Regular harvesting will encourage a bushier habit and will prevent plants from forming seed. Pinch as needed or cut back by half, starting from one end and moving through to the other, creating even growth.

SAFETY CONSIDERATIONS: Pregnant and nursing women should avoid taking it internally, as little evidence exists showing it is safe. Children can take small amounts internally. Do not use for two weeks before surgery, as it may cause drowsiness when taken with other medications. Avoid using it if you have thyroid disease.

PRESERVATION: Air-dry leaves, but don't dehydrate as essential oil content and aroma will deplete. Store in an airtight glass jar.

TIP: Lemon balm flowers attract bees. The word "melissa" in Greek means bees. If you have beehives, plant several plants nearby to feed the bees and help keep them calm while you open the hives.

KEEP IN MIND: Lemon balm contains 38 percent citronellal, an insect-repelling compound. Plant it where you sit outside and rub the leaves to release the compounds, helping repel mosquitoes.

TROUBLESHOOTING: Very few issues with insect pests. Cut back plants if they exhibit rust, powdery mildew, gray mold, or leaf blight. Dispose; don't compost.

LEMON VERBENA

(Aloysia triphylla)

Common name(s): lemon verbena or lemon beebrush

PARTS USED: Leaves and flowers

USES: Dry or fresh herbs can be used for tea. Leaves make a wonderful lemonade. They may be added to jams, cakes, and pies. Add fresh to fruit salad. Make a flavored vinegar by infusing with the leaves. They also make a great potpourri when dried and added to linen sachets.

Lemon verbena is beneficial for supporting digestion and relieving diarrhea and constipation. Drink lemon verbena tea to help reduce symptoms of the common cold and fever. Has sedative properties and can help with insomnia.

TASTE PROFILE: Lemony

GROWING: Can be grown from seed but will take years to reach maturity and achieve a harvest. Plants are usually grown from nursery stock. Perennial where winters are warm. In other areas, grow in a large pot and bring indoors before the first frost. Plants will grow to a height of two to four feet when grown in a container. In tropical climates, it will grow as an evergreen, reaching heights of ten to fifteen feet. When overwintered indoors, lemon verbena will lose its leaves as it enters dormancy.

ANNUAL OR PERENNIAL: Annual, unless overwintered indoors

LIGHT: Full sun

WATERING: Water regularly throughout the growing season. When moved indoors for the winter, reduce watering to a minimum and keep the pot in a bright, cool location.

SOIL: Light, well-draining loamy soil

ZONE: Native to Argentina and Chile, it is hardy in zones 8 to 10.

PRUNING: Prune growing tips in late summer, removing any spent flowers and encouraging a bushier habit.

COMPANIONS: Plant lemon verbena in a large planter. Over time, it will fill the pot, so only co-plant trailing herbs such as lemon thyme, or annual herbs such as lemon basil.

HARVESTING: Harvest leaves before they dry anytime during the growing season. Cut back individual branches when pruning.

SAFETY CONSIDERATIONS: Avoid using if pregnant or breastfeeding. If experiencing kidney problems, avoid taking large amounts as lemon verbena may irritate the kidneys and worsen kidney disease.

PRESERVATION: Dehydrate at a low temperature or lay leaves out to dry on racks until crispy. Entire branches may be tied into bunches with twine and hung upside down to dry. Store in an airtight glass container.

TIPS: Lemon verbena will root easily from softwood cuttings. Take cuttings in the spring to increase plant numbers.

KEEP IN MIND: When harvesting, wear long sleeves and gloves, because the oils in the leaves may cause irritation and dermatitis.

TROUBLESHOOTING: When grown in a greenhouse or indoors, lemon verbena may attract aphids, whiteflies, or spider mites. Spray them off with an insecticidal soap and use yellow sticky tape to trap them.

LEMONGRASS

(Cymbopogon citratus)

Common name(s): lemongrass

PARTS USED: Stem and leaves

USES: Lemongrass is used mainly as a flavoring in many Asian dishes. It is usually discarded before serving because it is very fibrous. Lemongrass can be used by itself or with other herbs to make tea. Lemongrass has antibacterial and antifungal properties that make it a great addition to homemade cleaning products. It also contains citronella oil and so can be used to repel mosquitoes. It also repels whiteflies.

TASTE PROFILE: Lemony

GROWING: If you want to seed lemongrass, keep in mind that germination may be very slow. Keep seeds moist and warm under a propagating dome (a clear plastic cover placed over seedlings to hold in moisture and warmth for better germination and growth). Start the seeds in early January. Lemongrass does well in containers either inside or outside. Plants will reach three feet tall. The easiest way to propagate lemongrass is to buy fresh stalks at an Asian grocery store and put them in a jar of water with the base of the stalk always submerged. After a few

days in a warm location, you should see roots forming. After about two weeks, transplant them into pots.

ANNUAL OR PERENNIAL: Perennial (if brought indoors in winter)

LIGHT: Full sun

WATERING: Lemongrass likes moist soil during the growing period. Containers should be watered daily, and gardens or raised beds should be watered two or three times per week.

SOIL: Lemongrass needs well-drained soil to thrive.

ZONE: Hardy in zones 10 to 11. In lower zones, grow it in a container and bring it indoors for the winter.

PRUNING: Lemongrass does not require pruning.

COMPANIONS: To achieve a better harvest, plant lemongrass in its own container because plants will fill out and roots will grow into a thick mass, outcompeting other plants growing nearby.

HARVESTING: Use pruners to cut stalks at the base when they are at least ½-inch thick.

SAFETY CONSIDERATIONS: Avoid taking lemongrass during pregnancy because it can promote menstrual flow. In rare cases, lemongrass oil may cause rashes. The blades are sharp, so take care when harvesting and wear gloves and long sleeves.

PRESERVATION: Lemongrass can be cut into pieces and dried in a cool, dark place or in a food dehydrator. Store dried lemongrass in glass jars for up to two years. You can also cut the top off the stalk pieces and freeze them in airtight freezer-safe bags for up to nine months.

TIP: Lemongrass can be divided in early spring and put into pots to make more plants.

MINT

(Mentha)

Common name(s): mint

PARTS USED: Leaves and flowers

USES: Mint leaves and flowers may be used to make a relaxing and refreshing tea, either hot or iced. Leaves are used frequently in Thai and Mediterranean cuisines. They are also used to flavor many desserts, chocolate, and drinks. Toss the leaves into fruit or vegetable salads.

Mint can help reduce tension headaches. Mint leaves can be chewed to freshen breath in lieu of breath mints. Drinking mint tea after a meal will help reduce abdominal pain and improve digestion.

TASTE PROFILE: Unique sweet flavor with a cooling sensation

GROWING: Generally, seeding is not recommended, especially because harvesting mint seeds is very difficult due to cross-pollination. If you decide to seed, make sure to buy seeds from a reputable supplier that has properly isolated the plants. It's easier to buy small plants from a nursery. Grows best in indoor or outdoor containers. Do not plant in the ground, because the roots will spread aggressively through your whole garden. Mint can easily be propagated from cuttings. Plants grow to one foot tall.

ANNUAL OR PERENNIAL: Perennial

LIGHT: Full sun to partial shade

WATERING: Mint prefers a moist environment, so make sure not to let the soil dry out between waterings. Keep watered during droughts.

SOIL: Mint enjoys a moist soil rich in organic matter.

ZONE: Hardy in zones 5 through 9

PRUNING: Remove flowers as they appear and prune back to six inches or so during early summer to encourage more leaf growth. Prune down to soil level in late fall or bring into the kitchen for winter growing. If any leaves show signs of rust, remove them immediately to stop the spread.

COMPANIONS: You will likely want to isolate mint in its own container because of its invasive nature.

HARVESTING: Using pruners or strong kitchen shears, cut the branches or pluck off leaves as needed.

SAFETY CONSIDERATIONS: Mint can cause heartburn and nausea. Do not take large medicinal amounts during pregnancy or while breastfeeding.

PRESERVATION: Mint can be dried in the oven, a food dehydrator, or by hanging upside down in a cool, dark place. Store dried mint in glass containers in a cool, dark place for one or two years.

TIP: If you don't want to plant mint in freestanding containers, you can cut the bottom out of a plastic five-gallon nursery container and bury it with just the rim above the surface of the soil. Plant mint in a pot to contain the roots.

TEA BUSH

(Camellia sinensis)

Common name(s): tea plant

PARTS USED: Leaves

USES: Tea leaves are used to make tea, whether white, green, black, or oolong. Recently, chefs have used tea leaves in baked goods, particularly Earl Grey.

Although all tea types have antioxidants, green tea has the highest levels and contains polyphenolic molecules called catechins. These catechins have anticancer properties. Tea leaves also contain an amino acid called L-theanine. Drinking tea helps improve heart health.

TASTE PROFILE: The flavor of the resulting tea is based on the type of tea brewed, length of brew, processing method after harvest, and region where it was grown. Generally, white tea has a delicate, sweet aroma and ranges in flavor from mildly sweet to grassy or nutty. Green tea can be floral, sweet, nutty, or vegetal. Black tea brewed at a lower temperature may be sweet and fruity, with a soft finish. Brewed at a higher temperature, it will seem thicker and richer, with deep malty, woody, and spicy notes. Less-oxidized oolongs tend to have a fruity, floral, or vegetal flavor, whereas more-oxidized oolongs tend to have a richer, deeper flavor with notes of spice and confectionary.

GROWING: *Camellia sinensis* grows best in a temperature range of 71°F to 85°F. Where summers are consistently 90°F or above, it is best to grow tea bushes in large containers and either move them to dappled shade or provide a shade covering. Where winters experience frost, grow camellia in a pot and move it indoors for the winter. *Camellia sinensis* grows best in a high-humidity environment, with high average rainfall.

ANNUAL OR PERENNIAL: Perennial

LIGHT: Full sun

WATERING: Minimum of two to four inches of water per week or more, depending on drought conditions. Water at the soil line, to prevent water splash on the leaves, and allow the top several inches of the soil to dry between waterings.

SOIL: Prefers acidic potting soil. Amend with sulfur or evergreen needles to lower the pH level.

ZONE: Hardy in zones 7 to 9. Grow in a container and move it indoors for the winter or where summers are too hot.

PRUNING: Cut plants back by four or five inches in the very early spring, before bud formation, to encourage new growth.

COMPANIONS: If growing in a container, grow *Camellia sinensis* on its own.

HARVESTING: Pinch back new growth, leaving older leaves and stems on the plant. For white tea, harvest the closed bud in the early spring, and possibly an additional top leaf. For green tea, harvest the top two just-opened leaves and the bud. Harvest the mature top two leaves and leaf bud for black tea, later in spring or summer. If harvesting oolong, harvest the top three leaves and leaf bud in either spring or summer.

SAFETY CONSIDERATIONS: Pregnant and nursing women should avoid drinking tea. Drinking too much caffeine may cause restlessness and anxiety, poor sleep, heartburn, headaches, and dizziness.

PRESERVATION: After the leaves have been harvested, they either need to be rolled or not to achieve the desired tea, then dried to stop oxidation. Once the leaves are fully dry, store them in an airtight glass jar, away from direct sunlight.

TIP: Fertilize with a diluted fish emulsion to encourage new growth.

KEEP IN MIND: To harvest tea leaves in a shorter amount of time, purchase mature tea plants. *Camellia sinensis* grown from seed will take at least three years to reach maturity.

TROUBLESHOOTING: *Camellia sinensis* is susceptible to aphids, scale insects, and spider mites. To prevent pests when grown indoors overwinter, use a humidifier near the plant and lower the ambient temperature.

TULSI BASIL / HOLY BASIL

(Ocimum tenuiflorum)

Common name(s): holy basil or tulsi

PARTS USED: Leaves and flowers

USES: Tulsi leaves make a wonderful tea. Leaves may be brewed on their own or blended with others. Stir-fry with chicken or beef and chile peppers for a delicious Thai-inspired dish.

Tulsi has been used to reduce stress, anxiety, high cholesterol, and elevated blood pressure. It has antibacterial and antiseptic properties. It is also used to support digestion, reduce fever, and boost the immune system.

TASTE PROFILE: Spicy clove flavor, hints of sweet mint, flowers, and black pepper

GROWING: Start new plants from seed or purchase starter plants. Germination may take two or three weeks. Sow seeds indoors, six weeks before the final frost date. Keep warm by setting over a heat mat or in a warm location until germination. Transplant to the garden after the final frost. Tulsi may be planted in a container or raised bed or in the ground. Plants will grow to a height and width of one or two feet.

ANNUAL OR PERENNIAL: Annual except where native (tropical regions)

LIGHT: Full sun

WATERING: Requires regular watering until established, then water when needed to maintain moisture.

SOIL: Prefers well-draining, loamy soil

ZONE: Hardy in zones 10b to 11

PRUNING: Allow plants to set flowers, then cut back by half before they dry. Plants will develop new stems from side branches and form a bushier habit.

COMPANIONS: Plant with other basil varieties because growing needs are similar. Will fill out and compete with large neighboring plants. Choose short, trailing plants such as creeping thyme, trailing rosemary, or sweet marjoram.

HARVESTING: Cut stems back by half, then pick off leaves and flowers. When grown as an annual, cut back the entire plant before the first frost.

SAFETY CONSIDERATIONS: Pregnant and breastfeeding women should avoid using tulsi basil. Avoid if you have hypothyroidism, because tulsi may lower thyroxine levels. Do not take two weeks before surgery, as it may slow blood clotting.

PRESERVATION: Dry entire stems by tying into bundles and hanging upside down. Air-dry on trays in a cool location, out of direct sunlight. Dehydrate at a low temperature until crispy. Store in an airtight glass container.

TIP: Plant tulsi in your vegetable garden to attract bees to pollinate fruiting crops.

KEEP IN MIND: Different from regular basil in taste and texture. I don't recommend using it for pesto or as a substitute for sweet basil.

TROUBLESHOOTING: Few pests are a problem. If you see aphids or Japanese beetles, spray with an insecticidal soap. Handpick Japanese beetles, then drop them into soapy water.

CHAPTER 4

Flowers

ANISE HYSSOP

(Agastache foeniculum)

Common name(s): anise hyssop

PARTS USED: Flowers and leaves

USES: Flowers and leaves may be dried for herbal tea or used fresh in salads. Dried flowers may be used for potpourri. Anise hyssop has been used to assist with digestive issues, skin conditions, and other health problems, but not enough evidence exists showing efficacy.

TASTE PROFILE: Sweet, mildly minty, soft licorice

GROWING: Start seeds indoors at least eight weeks before the final frost and transplant to the garden after the last frost. Seeds need light to germinate, so sow them on the surface of the seed-starting mix and cover with a thin layer of vermiculite. Transplant seedlings one or two feet apart. Anise hyssop will grow in raised beds or container gardens or in the ground. Plants spread by rhizomes and seeds. A member of the mint family, Lamiaceae, anise hyssop grows to a height of two to four feet and one to three feet wide.

ANNUAL OR PERENNIAL: Herbaceous perennial

LIGHT: Prefers full sun to partial shade

WATERING: Prefers medium to dry moisture level

SOIL: Will grow in average soil with good drainage

ZONE: Hardy in zones 4 to 9; native to the upper Midwest and Great Plains

PRUNING: Remove spent flowers or deadhead to encourage production of new blooms. Cut plants back by half and above a leaf joint. This will help create a bushier habit.

COMPANIONS: Pairs well with perennial herbs that prefer similar growing conditions, such as echinacea and bee balm. Annual chamomile makes a good companion.

HARVESTING: Both flowers and leaves are edible and can be harvested for tea. Leaves may be harvested at any time, whereas flowers are best harvested after they have fully formed and are bright purple.

SAFETY CONSIDERATIONS: Pregnant women should avoid using anise hyssop, because it may cause uterine contractions, leading to miscarriage. Not enough research exists showing safety for breastfeeding women.

PRESERVATION: Dry entire stems by tying into bunches and hanging upside down. Lay out in a dehydrator at a low temperature. Remove individual leaves and flowers and store in an airtight glass jar in a cool, dark place.

TIP: Flower seeds are attractive to birds. Any flowers left on the plant at the end of the season will provide a food source. Flowers are loved by bees, hummingbirds, and butterflies.

KEEP IN MIND: To control plant spread, plant anise hyssop in containers. Be sure to remove flower heads before they dry and drop seeds. Should plants self-seed, removal is easy.

TROUBLESHOOTING: Keep an eye out for root rot, which may develop when anise hyssop is grown in poorly draining soil. In humid environments, powdery mildew may develop.

BACHELOR BUTTONS

(Centaurea cyanus)

Common name(s): cornflower

PARTS USED: Flowers

USES: Bachelor buttons may be enjoyed in herbal teas, brewed on their own, or blended with other herbs. Often used in soap making and body care products. Freeze in ice cubes and add to iced tea or lemonade.

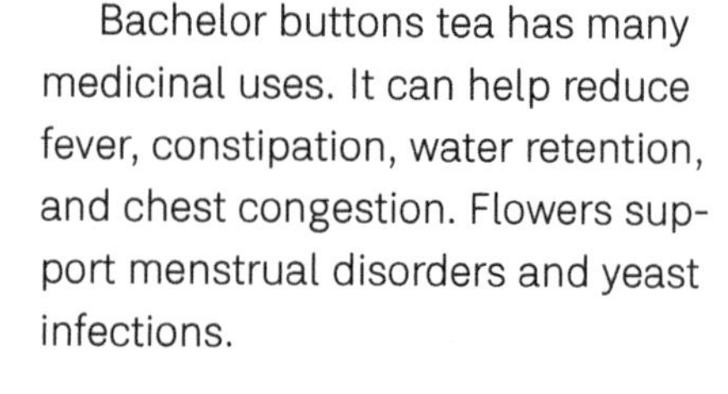

Bachelor buttons tea has many medicinal uses. It can help reduce fever, constipation, water retention, and chest congestion. Flowers support menstrual disorders and yeast infections.

TASTE PROFILE: Sweet and spicy, with a hint of clove

GROWING: Start seeds indoors, in seed trays, six to eight weeks before the final frost date. Pot up after they develop their first set of true leaves. Transplant to the garden after the last frost. Seeds can also be sown directly in the garden after the final frost. Plant at a depth of half an inch and cover with a thin layer of soil. Plants will grow to a height of one to three feet and up to one foot wide.

ANNUAL OR PERENNIAL: Annual

LIGHT: Full sun

WATERING: Maintain consistent moisture by watering regularly until established, then once a week.

SOIL: Prefers moist soil with good drainage but will grow in all soil types

ZONE: Grows as an annual everywhere except zones 8 to 10. Native to western Asia and Europe.

PRUNING: To prevent plants from dropping seeds, be sure to deadhead regularly.

COMPANIONS: Plant near calendula, bee balm, and other flowering herbs and plants. Plant in a vegetable garden to attract pollinators.

HARVESTING: Harvest in the morning and before the flowers fully open. The more you harvest, the more flowers will be produced, preventing seed development.

SAFETY CONSIDERATIONS: Avoid if you are pregnant or breastfeeding. Bachelor buttons may cause an allergic reaction if you have an allergy to ragweed.

PRESERVATION: Tie into bunches and hang upside down to dry, or use a dehydrator set at a low heat. Pinch off petals and store in an airtight glass jar in a cool, dark place.

TIP: There are many exciting colors available on the market. Plant many colors together and create a wild meadow effect.

KEEP IN MIND: *Centaurea cyanus* is different from *Centaurea montana*. The two are often mixed up, but *C. montana* is perennial, whereas *C. cyanus* is grown as an annual.

TROUBLESHOOTING: Plants may flop over because of insufficient light or insufficient water. If they are planted in full sun, give them more water. If they are planted in partial sun, next time, choose a full-sun location.

CALENDULA

(Calendula officinalis)

Common name(s): calendula, pot marigold

PARTS USED: Flowers and leaves

USES: Calendula makes a wonderful tea. It may be consumed on its own or blended with other herbs. Flowers have a healing effect on burns and rashes. Infuse olive oil with calendula blossoms, then strain the plant material out of the oil. You can apply the oil directly to the skin or use it as a base for salves and creams. Calendula flowers have antibacterial, antifungal, and antiseptic properties.

Dry calendula petals may be used in place of saffron. Add to rice; it provides a lovely orange hue. Add fresh petals to salads.

TASTE PROFILE: Dry flowers have a slightly bitter flavor. Brew at a lower temperature to release some of the sweeter notes.

GROWING: Calendula may be grown from seed. Start indoors four to six weeks before the final frost date or sow directly in the garden. Water well and maintain consistent moisture until established. Calendula may be grown in a container or raised bed or in the ground. Space plants fifteen inches apart. Plants will grow one and a half feet tall and wide.

ANNUAL OR PERENNIAL: Annual

LIGHT: Full sun

WATERING: Average watering, except during drought. Give calendula one or two inches of water per week.

SOIL: Will grow in most soil types but prefers good drainage and nutrients

ZONE: Grown as an annual, except in zones 9b to 11. Calendula is native to southern Europe and the eastern Mediterranean.

PRUNING: To maintain a bushy form and prevent self-seeding, prune back all spent flowers and seed heads. Cut at the base of the flower stem to keep a tidy form.

COMPANIONS: Calendula likes lavender, bachelor buttons, basil, and strawberries. Don't plant with dill, parsnips, or potatoes.

HARVESTING: In the morning, after the dew has evaporated, harvest calendula flowers by cutting below the flower heads. As you harvest, lay them out carefully in a garden basket to prevent damage.

SAFETY CONSIDERATIONS: Pregnant and nursing women should avoid calendula. If taking sedatives, avoid drinking calendula tea, as you may have unexpected interactions. You may have a reaction if you are allergic to ragweed and other members of the Asteraceae family.

PRESERVATION: Lay flowers out on a rack to air-dry or in a dehydrator at a low heat. Store in airtight glass jars in a cool, dark place.

TIP: Harvest flowers before they close and begin forming seeds.

KEEP IN MIND: Although the name "pot marigold" sounds like regular marigold, the two are not the same. Calendula is a member of the *Calendula* genus, whereas marigolds are a member of the *Tagetes* genus.

TROUBLESHOOTING: Calendula may be attacked by black aphids, leafhoppers, whiteflies, or blister beetles. For organic solutions, choose insecticidal soap or neem oil. Powdery mildew is common toward the end of summer. Stay on top of harvesting flowers and cut out affected plants at the base.

CHAMOMILE

(Matricaria recutita)

Common name(s): German chamomile

PARTS USED: Flowers

USES: Chamomile can be used in cooking; steep the flowers in hot water or infuse olive oil with the dry flowers. Fresh chamomile flowers add color and flavor to salads or can be steeped in cream to then use in dessert recipes.

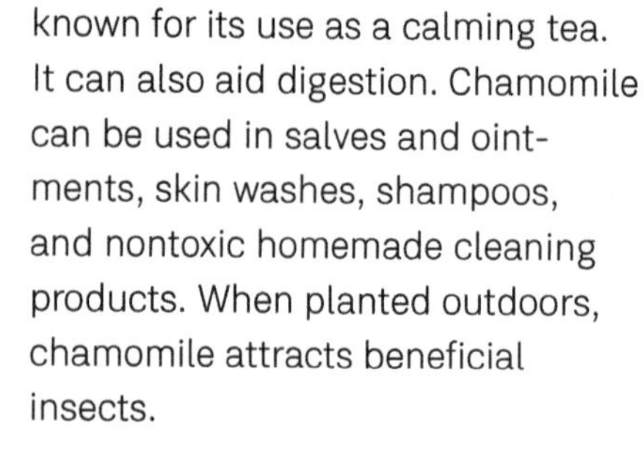

Chamomile is probably best known for its use as a calming tea. It can also aid digestion. Chamomile can be used in salves and ointments, skin washes, shampoos, and nontoxic homemade cleaning products. When planted outdoors, chamomile attracts beneficial insects.

TASTE PROFILE: Flowers have a sweet, herbaceous flavor but can get bitter if steeped for too long. To prevent this, steep at a lower temperature.

GROWING: Sow chamomile seeds directly in the garden or in the container where you plan to grow it. Grows equally well in indoor containers, in outdoor containers, in raised beds, and in the ground. Plants will grow to twelve to eighteen inches tall.

ANNUAL OR PERENNIAL: Annual, self-seeds easily

LIGHT: Tolerant of most conditions except full shade

WATERING: Keep the soil moist, an inch of water a week if growing in the ground.

SOIL: Chamomile will grow in any kind of soil, but it will do best in well-drained soil.

ZONE: It is fairly hardy and can grow in zones 3 to 9.

PRUNING: Do not prune other than harvesting the flower buds.

COMPANIONS: Grows well with other plants, especially onions. It's quite aggressive, and its self-seeding nature could choke off other plants, so keep it in check by hoeing where it's not wanted (if planted in the garden).

HARVESTING: Harvest flowers just before they fully open; you can likely get several harvests per summer.

SAFETY CONSIDERATIONS: Can cause allergic reactions if you are allergic to ragweed. Do not use it if you are taking blood thinners.

PRESERVATION: Dry flowers by laying them out in the sun on clean paper or a screen (be sure it's not too windy). You can also dry them in the oven or in a food dehydrator set at 95°F. Store in glass jars in a cool, dark place for up to one year.

TIP: Chamomile can be planted as a ground cover and is hardy enough to be walked upon.

BEE BALM / WILD BERGAMOT

(Monarda fistulosa)

Common name(s): bee balm or wild bergamot

PARTS USED: Leaves and flowers

USES: Use dry leaves or petals of bee balm in herbal tea blends. Fresh flowers and leaves may be added to salads. You can infuse apple cider vinegar with the dry leaves and petals. Jelly can be made from the flowers. Bee balm makes a refreshing addition to lemonade, agua fresca, or infused water. The leaves and flowers also can be used in baking bread or muffins.

Bee balm can be used to make a cooling salve, rinse, or poultice for use on minor burns or sunburns. It can be used to make a tea that is great for combating colds and flu or to treat indigestion. When planted outdoors, bee balm attracts bees and other pollinators.

TASTE PROFILE: Bee balm has a peppery flavor similar to oregano. Some varieties have a slight citrus flavor.

GROWING: Buy seedlings of bee balm instead of growing it from seed. Bee balm grows equally well in outdoor containers, in raised beds, and in the ground. It can be mildly invasive, so if that's a concern, opt for containers. Plants will grow to two to four feet tall.

ANNUAL OR PERENNIAL: Perennial

LIGHT: Full sun

WATERING: Soil should be kept evenly moist, but not too wet because bee balm is susceptible to powdery mildew. Make sure there is good air circulation around the plants to avoid powdery mildew.

SOIL: Plant bee balm in well-drained soil.

ZONE: Bee balm is fairly hardy and can grow in zones 3 through 9.

PRUNING: Pinch off dead flowers to promote more blooms. After the first frost, cut back to a couple of inches above the soil.

COMPANIONS: Bee balm grows well alongside annuals that enjoy similar conditions, such as basil, chives, and thyme. Bee balm also grows well with echinacea and St. John's wort.

HARVESTING: Harvest when the flowers are fully open. Keep on top of harvesting to promote more blooms.

SAFETY CONSIDERATIONS: Bee balm can promote menstruation and so should not be taken during pregnancy.

PRESERVATION: The leaves and flowers can be bundled and dried upside down in a cool, dark place, or they can be dried more quickly in a food dehydrator. Store dried bee balm in airtight glass jars in a cool, dark place for up to one year.

TIP: Even though it's also called bergamot (wild bergamot), bee balm is not what is used to make Earl Grey tea (bergamot tea). That tea is made from the oil of the citrus bergamot orange.

LAVENDER

(Lavandula angustifolia)

Common name(s): English lavender

PARTS USED: Flowers

USES: Lavender flowers can be used in many dishes, including desserts and cakes, breads, salad dressings, oils, and vinegars. It can be used in drinks such as lemonade and infused in alcohol. Lavender flowers added to herbal tea blends make a calming tea.

Lavender is well known for its calming and sedating qualities. A lavender bath before bed or a lavender sachet under your pillow can help you fall asleep faster. It can also be used in cleaning products as a natural fragrance.

TASTE PROFILE: Unique floral flavor, but can taste bitter or soapy if you use too much

GROWING: Seeds prefer cool temperatures to germinate. Either seed in the fall and leave in a cool greenhouse or cold frame (a shallow box, often wood, with a clear top that can be used outdoors to raise seedlings and protect small plants from cold and frost) over the winter, or sow in the spring in pots and put the pots in plastic bags in the freezer for up to one week. Hidcote lavender will germinate without cold treatment. Many varieties of lavender seedlings are available at garden centers. Lavender grows equally well in indoor or outdoor containers, in raised beds, and in the ground. Plants will reach three feet tall.

ANNUAL OR PERENNIAL: Perennial

LIGHT: Full sun

WATERING: Water sparingly only during drought conditions.

SOIL: Lavender requires well-draining soil and prefers a dry environment. Avoid fertilizing or amending the soil because lavender does better in poorer soils.

ZONE: In zone 5 and higher, it can be grown as a perennial. In zone 4 and lower, it can be grown as an annual.

PRUNING: Trim plants back in spring by no more than one-third as new growth begins, but avoid cutting back to the woody part of the plant. Trim plants in autumn as you did in the spring.

COMPANIONS: Grow lavender with plants of similar needs, such as echinacea and yarrow. It also does well with other Mediterranean herbs, including rosemary and thyme. Avoid planting near dill.

HARVESTING: Harvest flower stems by cutting with pruners or good kitchen scissors, just as flowers start to open.

SAFETY CONSIDERATIONS: Lavender can cause constipation, headache, and skin irritation. Lavender oil could cause hormonal imbalances in prepubescent boys. Stop taking any lavender two weeks before a scheduled surgery, and check with your doctor if pregnant or breastfeeding.

PRESERVATION: Dry flowers either on trays or hanging in bunches upside down. Keep them out of the sun to preserve the color. Dried lavender can retain its aroma for up to ten years. Store in an airtight container in a cool, dark place.

TIP: Seed starting can be tricky; another way to grow lavender is propagating via softwood cuttings in early summer and hardwood cuttings in the fall.

RED CLOVER

(Trifolium pratense)

Common name(s): red clover

PARTS USED: Flowers and sprouts

USES: Red clover is usually eaten as sprouts. Sprouts can be put on salads, sandwiches, and wraps and added to stir-fries.

The phytoestrogen in the flowers means that they can be used to make a sweet tea for treating menopausal symptoms. Red clover attracts beneficial insects.

TASTE PROFILE: Sprouts are nutty but mild; flowers taste and smell sweet.

GROWING: For sprouts: wash seeds well, soak for half a day, drain, and allow to sprout in a jar with a mesh top, washing seeds at least twice a day and draining. To seed red clover in soil, direct seed, and cover with a very thin layer of soil (less than ¼ inch). Red clover grows equally well in indoor or outdoor containers, in raised beds, and in the ground. Sprouts will grow to several inches long; mature plants in soil will reach fifteen inches tall.

ANNUAL OR PERENNIAL: Perennial down to zone 4

LIGHT: Full sun to partial shade

WATERING: Keep clover moist, especially in drought conditions.

SOIL: Good drainage is key for red clover. It also prefers slightly acidic soil (between pH 6.0 and 6.5).

ZONE: Red clover can survive winters down to zone 4.

PRUNING: Red clover does not require pruning.

COMPANIONS: Red clover is often used as a ground cover and spreads fairly rapidly due to self-seeding.

HARVESTING: For mature plants, harvest fully opened flowers in spring and summer; fall blossoms are not as sweet. You can keep sprouts in the refrigerator for a few days and remove as many as you need.

SAFETY CONSIDERATIONS: Because clover acts like estrogen and could cause hormone imbalances, it's not recommended during pregnancy, if breastfeeding, if you have cancers of the reproductive organs, or if you have a protein S deficiency. It can also increase the chance of bleeding if you have a bleeding disorder. Do not use it for two weeks prior to a scheduled surgery.

PRESERVATION: Flowers can be dried in a dehydrator at 115°F or laid out on a tray or rack until fully dry. Store in an airtight glass jar, out of direct sunlight.

TIP: Red clover can be used as a cover crop to improve soil. It helps add nitrogen to the soil. It can break up heavy soils and help prevent erosion from wind and rain. It's also often used as animal feed.

ROSELLE/HIBISCUS

(Hibiscus sabdariffa)

Common name(s): roselle, hibiscus, Jamaica sorrel

PARTS USED: Flower calyxes

USES: Many herbal teas include roselle for its red color and tart, lemony flavor. Roselle tea can be brewed hot or cold and blended with other ingredients. It is loved in Jamaican and Caribbean cuisine, added to soups, salads, and meat and vegetable dishes. It makes a wonderful jam and delicious beverage.

Roselle is high in vitamin C and vitamin A and antioxidants. Roselle tea helps reduce high blood pressure.

TASTE PROFILE: Tart, lemony, and mildly sweet

GROWING: Where winters experience a freeze, start seeds indoors at least three months before the last frost. Plant in the garden after the risk of frost has passed. In zones 9 to 12, seeds are sown directly in well-drained garden soils. Roselle can be grown in a raised bed or in the ground. Consider planting in a container then moving it indoors for the winter. In tropical climates, roselle can grow to a height of seven feet.

ANNUAL OR PERENNIAL: Perennial in tropical climates, annual elsewhere

LIGHT: Full sun

WATERING: Requires moderate watering, at least once a week

SOIL: Well-draining, nutrient-rich soil

ZONE: Hardy in zones 9 to 12. Roselle is perennial in tropical climates but is usually grown as an annual.

PRUNING: No pruning required. Remove flower calyxes after the flower has faded and the calyx has swollen.

This approach will produce more flowers.

COMPANIONS: In warm climates, plants will grow tall and possibly shade out companions. In cooler climates, it will be shorter. Pair with basil, calendula, and tulsi basil.

HARVESTING: Harvest after the flowers have withered and the seedpods within the calyxes are swollen but tender. This is usually seven to ten days after flowers have withered. Use garden snips to remove each flower, because a second calyx is directly behind.

SAFETY CONSIDERATIONS: Pregnant and breastfeeding women should avoid consuming roselle. Stop using two weeks prior to surgery, because it might affect blood sugar.

PRESERVATION: Before drying, slice open each calyx and remove the seed capsule. Place in a dehydrator and dry at a low temperature. Store in an airtight glass jar in a cool, dark place.

TIP: Let a few calyxes mature for seed saving. Use those seeds to start a new crop the following year.

KEEP IN MIND: Roselle seeds may take a while to germinate. Consider germinating in a damp paper towel, sealed inside a plastic zip-top bag. Once seeds germinate, remove and pot up into four-inch pots.

TROUBLESHOOTING: Be sure to weed regularly to prevent competing plants from shading out young roselle plants and thereby stunting their growth.

SWEET VIOLET

(Viola odorata)

Common name(s): sweet violet, English violet

PARTS USED: Flowers and leaves

USES: Flowers and leaves may be used in tea. Sweet violet flowers will turn your tea a turquoise color. If you add a splash of lemon juice to the tea, the color will change to purple. Flowers may be candied or cooked into a flower syrup. Add raw flowers to salads, along with the young spring leaves. Freeze flowers in ice cubes. The leaves of sweet violet are high in vitamin C and vitamin A, are anti-inflammatory, and have been used to support bronchitis, breaking up phlegm.

TASTE PROFILE: Flowers smell and taste sweet and floral.

GROWING: If growing from seed, plant in a little soil, cover with plastic, and set inside the refrigerator for three months (they need time at a cold temperature before they will germinate). After treatment, plant seeds into a seed tray and pot up once they germinate and grow. Select a partially shady, moist in-ground location and transplant the seedlings fifteen to eighteen inches apart. To control spread, consider planting in a large container or pot. Plants will grow as a ground cover, only reaching six to eight inches tall and one or two feet wide.

ANNUAL OR PERENNIAL: Perennial

LIGHT: Partial sun to dappled shade; imagine a bright forest floor.

WATERING: Prefers moist soil. Water in drought conditions.

SOIL: Will grow in any type of well-draining soil.

ZONE: Hardy in zones 4 to 8; the sweet violet is native to Europe.

PRUNING: Flowers will appear in the early spring. Remove spent flowers to control seed drop. Plants will spread by underground rhizomes. Divide and split plants in the fall to prevent them from overtaking an area.

COMPANIONS: Sweet violets should be grown on their own because they tend to choke out neighboring plants. Grow in a container or select an area where plants may grow unrestricted.

HARVESTING: Harvest flowers in the spring when they are fresh. Gently pull, and the flowers will come up with a thin stem. Snip young leaves as needed.

SAFETY CONSIDERATIONS: Pregnant and breastfeeding women should avoid consuming sweet violets; there isn't enough information showing it is safe.

PRESERVATION: Air-dry the flowers on a tray or plate until fully dry or dehydrate at 95°F. Store in an airtight glass container in a cool, dark place.

TIP: Add dry flowers to tea or combine with other herbs to add color and health benefits.

KEEP IN MIND: *Viola tricolor,* also known as pansies, are different from sweet violets. Although both flowers are edible, pansies are cultivated annuals, whereas sweet violets are perennials.

TROUBLESHOOTING: Sweet violets growing in full sun may not produce as many flowers or grow as well as those planted in partial shade. If you live in a location where summers tend to be cool, a full-sun location will be appropriate.

CHAPTER 5

Fruits and Seeds

BLACK CURRANT

(Ribes nigrum)

Common name(s): black currant

PARTS USED: Fruit and leaves

USES: Black currants make a delicious jam, jelly, or syrup. Dried berries and leaves make a flavorful tea and can be blended with other ingredients.

Black currants are high in vitamin C and rich in antioxidants called anthocyanins. Anthocyanins have anti-inflammatory, antidiabetic, and antiaging properties and help prevent cardiovascular illness.

TASTE PROFILE: Fully ripe black currants are strongly aromatic and have a tart, rich flavor.

GROWING: Black currant bushes are deciduous, losing their leaves in the fall. Select a permanent location for planting in the ground, in a raised bed, in or in a large container. Prepare the soil by adding a two-inch layer of compost and gently raking it in. Dig a hole, add a handful of worm castings, then water in well. Transplant no deeper than the level of the nursery grown pot. Space plants four feet apart. Plants will grow to a height and width of three or four feet. Peak fruit production is reached in the fourth year.

ANNUAL OR PERENNIAL: Perennial

LIGHT: Full sun to partial shade

WATERING: Prefers regular moisture; won't tolerate drought. Keep consistently moist until established.

SOIL: Grows best in well-draining, nutrient-rich soil.

ZONE: Hardy in zones 3 to 7. In warmer zones, plant in afternoon shade.

PRUNING: It is best to leave pruning until the end of winter. Cut out crossing and dead stems and trim back inward-facing branches and crossing or broken branches.

COMPANIONS: Black currants grow best with plants preferring similar growing conditions. Raspberries and gooseberries make good companions. Choose trailing or low-growing herbs for understory plantings, such as lemon balm, oregano, thyme, and trailing lavender.

HARVESTING: Black currants are ready for harvest by midsummer. Harvest individual berries or entire clusters once berries ripen to full black.

SAFETY CONSIDERATIONS: Pregnant and breastfeeding women should avoid using black currants due to a lack of research showing they are safe. Avoid using it if you have a bleeding disorder, as it may increase the risk of bruising or bleeding. Stop using two weeks prior to surgery, as it might slow blood clotting.

PRESERVATION: Berries may be frozen whole or dehydrated at 115°F. Store dried berries in an airtight glass jar.

TIP: Black currants are self-fertile. Only one plant is needed to produce fruit.

KEEP IN MIND: Keep an eye on berries as they ripen so you can pick them before birds eat them.

TROUBLESHOOTING: Black currants can be a host for white pine blister rust, typically a fatal disease of white pines. Some states have banned growing all species of *Ribes*. Check with your local extension office before purchasing.

BLUEBERRY

(Vaccinium corymbosum)

Common name(s): highbush blueberry

PARTS USED: Fruit

USES: Dried berries can be added to tea blends, and frozen berries can be used for iced tea. Blueberries are often used in baking (e.g., muffins and pies) or cooked into jams, jellies, and syrups.

Blueberries are high in antioxidants and vitamins A, C, E, and K. They are used to help lower cholesterol, control blood pressure spikes, boost the immune system, and improve digestion.

TASTE PROFILE: Sweet; slightly tart when unripe

GROWING: Plant at least two blueberry plants for fruit pollination. Two different varieties will ensure a larger crop. Although a single plant is self-fertile, you will guarantee a larger harvest when two different varieties are planted near each other. In areas where the soil is not acidic, grow blueberries in containers. It is easier to purchase acidic potting soil than it is to amend in-ground alkaline soil.

ANNUAL OR PERENNIAL: Perennial

LIGHT: Full sun to partial shade

WATERING: Don't allow the soil to dry out; blueberries prefer a consistently moist soil.

SOIL: Well-draining, nutrient-rich, acidic soil

ZONE: Hardy in zones 5 to 8

PRUNING: Prune at the end of the growing season by cutting down last year's fruiting stems to the base. Trim back brown tips to the first forming bud.

COMPANIONS: None

HARVESTING: Harvest blueberries in the early morning before the heat of day reduces their freshness.

SAFETY CONSIDERATIONS: Stop eating blueberries two weeks prior to surgery, to help control blood glucose levels.

PRESERVATION: There are many ways to preserve blueberries. For tea purposes, use a dehydrator set at 115°F to 120°F. Consider pretreating by dipping berries in boiling water, then dunking in cold water. This will decrease dehydration time and prevent the skin from breaking. Berries will be pliable, not wet. Store in an airtight glass jar. Frozen berries may be used to make iced tea.

TIP: Birds love blueberries and will snatch them before harvesttime if you are not vigilant about picking berries as they ripen.

KEEP IN MIND: When plants begin outgrowing their current container, select the next size pot and fill with acidic potting soil. Make a well in the center, water, and transplant the blueberry plant. Firm in around the top.

TROUBLESHOOTING: If leaves are yellowing, this is most likely chlorosis caused by plants growing in alkaline soil. To solve this, grow blueberry plants in containers and only use acidic potting soil. Add a two-inch layer of peat moss or pine bark to help maintain pH levels.

ELDERBERRY

(Sambucus canadensis)

Common name(s): elder, elderberry

PARTS USED: Fruit and flowers

USES: Dry elderberries and flowers can be used for tea. Flowers make a nice cordial.

Elderberries are high in vitamin A and vitamin C, antioxidants, phosphorus, potassium, and iron. The antiviral properties in the berries help boost the immune system. A syrup of elderberry juice and honey can be taken preventatively and as a cough syrup.

TASTE PROFILE: Berries shouldn't be eaten raw because their seeds are toxic. Preserved berries are sweet.

GROWING: Plant nursery-grown elderberry plants, because it takes at least one year for plants to establish. Remove any weeds and plant in a raised bed or in the ground, spaced at least six feet apart. Mulch deeply with wood chips or straw to prevent weed competition. Plants will grow five to ten feet tall and six feet wide.

ANNUAL OR PERENNIAL: Perennial

LIGHT: Prefers full sun

WATERING: Provide one or two inches of water per week in the first year, then hand water or irrigate if conditions are dry.

SOIL: Well-draining, moist soil amended with organic matter. Will tolerate any soil type as long as it is well-draining.

ZONE: Hardy in zones 5 to 7

PRUNING: Prune in the late winter before buds show signs of breaking. Cut out three-year-old canes and dead or diseased canes, and thin plants to eight canes to increase airflow. New canes will grow in the spring.

COMPANIONS: Elderberry grows well with plants of similar growing requirements, such as currants and blueberries.

HARVESTING: Harvest fully open flowers. Wait until berries are purplish black, harvesting only ripe fruit with no signs of green.

SAFETY CONSIDERATIONS: All parts of the elderberry plant are toxic except the pulp and juice. Remove

all stems, leaves, and seeds before cooking.

PRESERVATION: Berries can be frozen, dried in a dehydrator at 135°F, or processed immediately into a syrup and refrigerated for up to six months. Flowers may be air dried or dehydrated at 95°F. Store in an airtight glass jar in a cool, dark place.

TIP: If birds are a problem, consider harvesting elderflowers for tea. They have a mild, floral, and fruity flavor.

KEEP IN MIND: The easiest way to remove berries from stems is with a comb or fork. Holding the berry cluster over a large bowl, gently run the comb through the stems and the berries will fall off.

TROUBLESHOOTING: Infestation by spotted wing drosophila is becoming a problem among elderberries. Flies will lay their eggs in developing fruit and larvae will hatch, infesting them. Keep an eye on ripe fruit clusters that fall to the ground, which is a sign of their presence. To prevent infestation in the first year, cover plants with a 1mm mesh netting or use nylon socks over berry clusters.

GOJI BERRY

(Lycium barbarum)

Common name(s): goji berry, wolfberry

PARTS USED: Fruit

USES: Add dried goji berries to herbal tea blends for a sweet flavor. Fresh or dry berries can be eaten raw, added to salads, oatmeal, or smoothies. Add to nuts and seed mixes.

Goji berries are high in vitamins A and C, antioxidants, and beta-carotene. They help stabilize blood sugar, improve anxiety and depression, and prevent liver damage.

TASTE PROFILE: Fresh berries have a mild, sweet flavor, with a hint of red pepper or cherry tomato. Dried berries are sweet and chewy, resembling a raisin.

GROWING: Goji berry is a member of the Solanaceae family and is cousins with the tomato. Best grown from nursery stock, because plants take at least one year to establish and two years to produce fruit. Plant after the last spring frost, spaced three to five feet apart. Water regularly until established. Pruned plants can grow to a height of three to six feet; left unpruned they will grow up to twelve feet tall.

ANNUAL OR PERENNIAL: Perennial

LIGHT: Full sun

WATERING: Moderate watering; too much water may encourage rot and not enough may cause blossom end rot. Mulch after planting to maintain moisture and prevent weeds.

SOIL: Prefers a well-drained loamy soil, light in texture

ZONE: Hardy in zones 5 to 9

PRUNING: Goji berry is a deciduous shrub, meaning it drops its leaves in the fall. Prune at the end of winter to control plant height, thin out main stems to improve air circulation, remove dead branches, and shorten lateral branches.

COMPANIONS: Plant goji berry with calendula, basil, catnip, and mint. Don't plant with fennel, ginger, or turmeric.

HARVESTING: Berries are ready for harvest by midsummer when they are bright red and easily fall off. Harvest by hand, removing one berry at a time. Be gentle; damaged berries spoil quickly.

SAFETY CONSIDERATIONS: Goji berries may cause the uterus to contract. Pregnant and breastfeeding women should avoid it. Avoid if you are allergic to tomatoes, peaches, nuts, or tobacco.

PRESERVATION: Pick through the berries and remove leaves, stems, and damaged or rotting fruit, then rinse well. Dehydrate at 140°F on lined racks until berries are fully dry and firm. Store in an airtight glass jar in a cool, dark place.

TIP: Consider using a trellis to support plants and prevent them from flopping over. This will keep fruit clean and off the ground.

TROUBLESHOOTING: Be sure to wear thick gardening gloves and long sleeves to protect arms during pruning. As plants mature, they develop spines along the older stems. Remove older stems but leave a few spines to protect crops from birds.

LEMON

(Citrus limon)

Common name(s): lemon

PARTS USED: Fruit

USES: Dried lemon peel can be added to tea blends, and a slice of lemon will brighten and balance bitter tea. Lemonade is made by mixing lemon and sugar and adding it to water. Lemon zest is often used in recipes. Lemons are used for cleaning, disinfecting, and degreasing.

High in vitamins C and B, calcium, and niacin. Lemons help break up congestion and phlegm. Add a few slices to tea for colds and flus, or drink in a glass of water in the morning as a detox or before a meal. Lemon juice may help reduce kidney stones, assist with weight loss, and improve digestive health.

TASTE PROFILE: Sour, tart, and juicy

GROWING: In a tropical climate, lemon trees can be planted in garden soil. Where winters are cold, grow dwarf lemon trees in containers and bring them indoors to overwinter. Choose a large clay pot for air circulation and drainage. Fertilize with a citrus fertilizer when plants are in active growth. Container-grown lemon trees can reach six feet, but the pot will control growth and root expansion.

ANNUAL OR PERENNIAL: Perennial

LIGHT: Minimum of eight to twelve hours of full sun.

WATERING: Outdoor plants need a minimum of two inches per week. Water indoor plants when the top two inches of the soil feel dry. Do not overwater or plants may become waterlogged, attracting pests or losing their leaves.

SOIL: Moist, well-draining, slightly acidic soil

ZONE: Hardy in zones 9b to 13b; lemon trees have trouble recovering if exposed to frost.

PRUNING: Prune trees, keeping them under ten feet tall. Indoor or container-grown trees can be cut back to a shorter, more manageable height. Roots may be cut back slightly to avoid the need for potting up to a larger container.

COMPANIONS: Plant basil, rosemary, lavender, or calendula at the base of lemon trees.

HARVESTING: Lemons are ready for harvest when the skin ripens to yellow and becomes glossy and fruits feel less firm.

SAFETY CONSIDERATIONS: When consumed as food, lemons are considered safe for pregnant and breastfeeding women.

PRESERVATION: Lemon peel or slices can be dehydrated at 120°F until dry. Store in an airtight glass jar.

TIP: Lemon trees will develop thorns along the leaf joint. Snip them off when needed and it won't harm the plants.

KEEP IN MIND: Container-grown lemon trees will shed up to 75 percent of developing fruit and only maintain what they can support.

TROUBLESHOOTING: If fungus gnats are a problem, cover the soil with a thick layer of vermiculite to prevent the gnats from laying eggs and use yellow sticky traps to catch adult gnats.

RASPBERRY

(Rubus idaeus)

Common name(s): raspberry

PARTS USED: Fruit and leaves

USES: Fresh or dried berries and leaves can be used for tea. Make iced tea from fresh berries. Raspberries are commonly used in baking, jams, jellies, syrups, sorbet, and smoothies. Fresh berries are lovely on yogurt, cereal, or oatmeal.

Raspberries are high in vitamin C, B vitamins, potassium, manganese, omega-3 fatty acids, antioxidants, and fiber. Raspberry leaf has been used to help calm an upset stomach and assist with colds and flus.

TASTE PROFILE: Berries have a sweet, rich, tart flavor. Leaves are mild and can be mixed with other herbal tea ingredients.

GROWING: Raspberry cultivars are available in red, yellow, black, or purple. Choose a spot in the garden, in a raised bed, or in a large container for the raspberry canes, and dig a hole slightly deeper than nursery grown. Space plants at least two or three feet apart. Plants will grow to a height and width of three to nine feet.

ANNUAL OR PERENNIAL: Plants are perennial, whereas each cane is biennial, meaning it only lives for two years.

LIGHT: Full sun to partial shade

WATERING: Give plants one and a half inches of water per week, from flowering to harvest.

SOIL: Well-draining soil, rich in organic matter. Soil that holds water may rot plant roots.

ZONE: Hardy in zones 4 to 8

PRUNING: Remove raspberry canes after harvesting by cutting them down to ground level. Cut out damaged or weakened canes in the early spring and shorten canes to four feet for easier harvest.

COMPANIONS: Plant with echinacea and currants as a plant support.

HARVESTING: Harvest berries as they ripen, easily falling off the core. Place berries in a shallow plate or basket without stacking. Refrigerate or process immediately to prevent spoilage.

SAFETY CONSIDERATIONS: Some research says to avoid using red raspberry leaf during and after pregnancy, although other sources say it is beneficial. Before using, do your own research and speak to a healthcare provider.

If you have hormone-sensitive cancers, endometriosis, or uterine fibroids, red raspberry leaf may act as an estrogen. Avoid it if your condition is sensitive to estrogen.

PRESERVATION: Dry berries and leaves in a dehydrator at 115°F. Leaves may also be air dried. Store leaves and fruit in separate airtight glass containers.

TIP: Raspberry plants produce fruit on floricanes, which are second-year primocanes. After floricanes bear fruit, they will die and can be cut down.

KEEP IN MIND: First-year plants won't produce fruit until their second year.

TROUBLESHOOTING: Although not required, a trellis system helps support plant growth, improves air circulation, and makes harvesting easier.

ROSEHIP

(Rosa rugosa)

Common name(s): Rugosa rose

PARTS USED: Fruit

USES: Rosehips are the fruit of the rose plant. When roses flower and go to seed, they produce rosehips, which are commonly used in teas, syrups, or jelly.

High in vitamins C, E, and B1, calcium, magnesium, and antioxidants. Rosehips may be used to support the immune system and prevent colds and flus. Helps relieve osteoarthritis and pain after surgery.

TASTE PROFILE: Floral, citrus, tangy with a slight bitterness

GROWING: Rugosa rose can be planted in the ground or a container. If grown in a large pot or container, choose a pot two times the size of the root ball and just as deep. Amend the potting soil with worm castings, and water it well.

ANNUAL OR PERENNIAL: Perennial

LIGHT: Full sun

WATERING: Container-grown roses need daily watering until established. Roses planted in the ground need moderate watering, based on the amount of rainwater received.

SOIL: Well-draining soil but will grow in most soil types

ZONE: Hardy in zones 2 to 7

PRUNING: Does not require pruning, except to remove dead or diseased branches and stems.

COMPANIONS: Due to the growth habit and thorny nature, companion planting is not recommended.

HARVESTING: In the late summer, any flowers left on the plant will have been pollinated and gone to seed, developing rosehips. They are ready for harvest when they mature from green to an orange or red color. Snip rosehips off just below the fruit and bring indoors. Rosehips can be used raw or dried.

SAFETY CONSIDERATIONS: Pregnant and breastfeeding women should avoid using rosehips as medicine, but food use is considered safe. Consuming large amounts of rosehips can lead to kidney stones, due to the high vitamin C content.

PRESERVATION: Trim furry tops from each rosehip, then slice open to remove the seed capsule and hairs. Dry at the lowest oven setting, moving them around every five minutes, until flesh is a dark color and hard. Store in an airtight glass jar.

TIP: Rugosa rose will grow well in sandy soil and is often used as a beach hedge, preventing erosion. If your soil is sandy, consider planting rugosa rose directly in the garden, because it requires little maintenance.

KEEP IN MIND: Take care when working with plants; the stems are covered in very sharp thorns. Be sure to wear thick gloves and long sleeves to prevent injury.

TROUBLESHOOTING: To prevent the plants from spreading by suckers and forming a thick hedge, grow the plants in large containers.

STRAWBERRY

(Fragaria spp.)

Common name(s): strawberry

PARTS USED: Fruit, leaves, and flowers

USES: Strawberries make a beautiful addition to the garden. They may be eaten raw, cooked into a jam, or baked into tasty desserts. Freeze and add whole to smoothies, use instead of ice cubes, or puree and freeze for a sorbet. Dice, dehydrate, and add to tea blends, mix into oatmeal, or sprinkle over yogurt and granola.

Very high in antioxidants, strawberries are also high in vitamin C, vitamin B_9 (folate), potassium, manganese, and fiber.

TASTE PROFILE: When ripe, flavor is sweet, juicy, and fragrant.

GROWING: A member of the rose family (Rosaceae), strawberries may be grown from seed. Start seeds ten to twelve weeks before the final frost date and transplant after the last spring frost. Cultivars are divided into two categories: June-bearing and everbearing. June-bearing varieties produce all their fruit by June or late spring, whereas everbearing varieties begin cropping in the spring and produce fruit until frost at six-week intervals. Plants grow to about eight inches tall.

ANNUAL OR PERENNIAL: Perennial

LIGHT: Plants require a minimum of six to eight hours of full sun.

WATERING: A moderate amount of watering is required, primarily at planting time. Once plants establish, avoid watering the fruit, because too much moisture may cause them to rot. Consider applying a layer of straw to keep the berries clean and dry.

SOIL: Well-draining and compost rich

ZONE: Hardy in zones 4 to 9. If growing outside, select a sunny spot away from trees, with good airflow.

PRUNING: After planting, remove developing flowers for several weeks to redirect growth energy into root development. Remove runners during the growing season.

COMPANIONS: Plant strawberries with borage, lettuce, chives, and parsley. Do not plant next to brassicas because they will compete for nutrients.

HARVESTING: Harvest when berries are fully red. Berries won't keep, so refrigerate or process immediately after harvest.

SAFETY CONSIDERATIONS: Avoid if allergic to fruit in the Rosaceae family.

PRESERVATION: Strawberries may be dehydrated or used fresh in tea. If using fresh berries, add fruit slices to a cold brew. If drying, dice and dehydrate at 130°F for ten to twelve hours or until fully dry but pliable. When fruit feels dry, store in a glass jar in a cool, dark place for one or two years.

KEEP IN MIND: Consider growing an alpine or wild strawberry variety, which have a richer flavor and are not available in stores.

TROUBLESHOOTING: If squirrels are a problem, cover the plants with a sheer row cover or mesh bags when fruits begin to set.

CHAPTER 6

Roots

CHICORY

(Cichorium intybus)

Common name(s): blue sailors, blue dandelion, succory, coffeeweed

PARTS USED: Roots, flowers, and leaves

USES: Chicory roots, flowers, and leaves can be used to make medicinal tea. For tea, make a decoction with 2 teaspoons of dry root in 2 cups of water. Simmer for at least fifteen minutes and add flowers and leaves in the last three minutes. For a caffeine-free coffee, bake roots at 350°F, grind in a coffee grinder, and brew like coffee.

Chicory is high in vitamin C, B vitamins, vitamin K, and beta-carotene. Drinking chicory tea will aid with digestion, act as a mild laxative, decrease swelling, and help absorb calcium. Chicory helps reduce cholesterol and assists with weight loss.

TASTE PROFILE: Rich, creamy, woody, nutty, resembling coffee

GROWING: Plants spread easily by seeds or roots; it is best to plant chicory in a large pot or container to control the spread. If growing plants from seed, select a suitable location and sow seeds directly where you want them to grow. From the second year onward, chicory plants will produce edible sky-blue flowers. Plants will grow to a height of three or four feet and width of two feet. Remove stray or unwanted plants.

ANNUAL OR PERENNIAL: Perennial

LIGHT: Prefers a full-sun location

WATERING: Water until established, then very little.

SOIL: Well-draining soil; loamy loose soil is best for growing roots.

ZONE: Hardy in zones 3 to 9

PRUNING: No pruning required; cut back plants at the end of the season.

COMPANIONS: Plant with fennel. Don't plant with other chicory varieties because they attract similar pests.

HARVESTING: Harvest in the early fall when plants start dying back. Pull up entire plants with roots. Cut off stems and brush off any loose soil. Wash roots thoroughly using a hard brush, removing as much dirt as possible.

SAFETY CONSIDERATIONS: Pregnant and breastfeeding women should only use food amounts of chicory and avoid using it for medicine. Chicory may lower blood sugar levels if you have diabetes. Increases bile production. If you have gallstones, using chicory may worsen them. Avoid using chicory two weeks prior to surgery.

PRESERVATION: Peel roots carefully as they can be tough. Slice roots, lay out on a baking sheet, and dry in an oven set at 212°F until thoroughly dry. Store in an airtight glass jar.

TIP: Plants will grow wild in open fields and roadsides. Chicory may be foraged when grown in a chemical-free location.

KEEP IN MIND: Bees and pollinators love chicory flowers. Grow chicory in your vegetable garden and where you want to attract pollinators.

TROUBLESHOOTING: Chicory has few pests.

ECHINACEA

(Echinacea purpurea)

Common name(s): coneflower, purple coneflower

PARTS USED: Roots, flowers, and leaves

USES: Make a decoction with the roots. Simmer 1½ teaspoons of echinacea root for at least fifteen minutes in 2 cups of water. Strain or infuse with dry petals and a pinch of leaves. Before drinking, strain for a healthy, relaxing tea.

Echinacea tea is beneficial for colds and flus, taken at the first sign of symptoms. Regular use will help strengthen the immune system and fight off infections.

TASTE PROFILE: Earthy, strong, floral

GROWING: Purchase nursery-grown plants or sow echinacea seeds directly in the garden. It is best grown in the ground and requires little attention after establishment. Plants will grow to a height of two to five feet.

ANNUAL OR PERENNIAL: Perennial

LIGHT: Prefers full sun to partial shade

WATERING: Once established, echinacea requires little watering. In the first year, water one or two inches per week to help establish roots. If grown in wet conditions, gauge by amount of rainfall and supplement watering when needed.

SOIL: Well-draining soil but will grow in most soil types

ZONE: Hardy in zones 3 to 8

PRUNING: Prune back plants to ground level in the spring. Dry flowers will feed birds over winter.

COMPANIONS: Plant with other perennials that attract pollinators, such as bee balm, catmint, lavender, lemon balm, anise hyssop, and tulsi basil.

HARVESTING: Flowers and leaves can be harvested at any time. Roots are best harvested in the early fall. Dig up a portion of the root and remove as much of the soil as possible.

SAFETY CONSIDERATIONS: Pregnant women can safely take echinacea for up to seven days. Breastfeeding women should avoid it. Don't take it if you have an autoimmune disease, as it may worsen your condition. Don't take echinacea if drinking caffeine, as it may increase caffeine levels in the body.

PRESERVATION: Wash roots thoroughly. Leave to air-dry, then chop into pieces. Dehydrate at 115°F until hard. Flowers and leaves may be dehydrated at 105°F. Store roots separately from flowers and leaves in airtight glass jars.

TIP: Plants must be three years mature to achieve a harvest. A nursery-grown plant will save you at least one or two years, achieving a harvest sooner than if grown from seed.

KEEP IN MIND: There are two other species of echinacea that may be grown for tea, both with medicinal benefits; *Echinacea angustifolia* and *Echinacea pallida. Echinacea purpurea* has the sweetest scent of the three.

TROUBLESHOOTING: Many of the new hybrid echinacea varieties available in bright colors of red, orange, and yellow are not as hardy as *E. purpurea* and have sterile seeds. If you want to grow echinacea for its medicinal benefits, only grow the species mentioned here.

GINGER

(Zingiber officinale)

Common name(s): gingerroot

PARTS USED: Roots and leaves

USES: Ginger is used in cuisines around the world, and its pungent flavor makes a refreshing drink. Dried or fresh ginger is delicious in tea and can be blended with other ingredients. Make iced tea with sliced ginger and honey.

Ginger helps relieve arthritis pain and acts as an anti-inflammatory. Use it to help reduce nausea and morning sickness and as a digestive aid. Ginger has been used to boost the immune system and is high in vitamins B and C, magnesium, iron, and calcium.

TASTE PROFILE: Spicy, pungent, lemony, sweet

GROWING: Ginger is similar to turmeric in growth and takes at least eight months to achieve a harvest. Grow in a raised bed or large container garden. Where winters are cold, grow in a pot then bring indoors for the winter. Purchase organic ginger rhizomes with swollen bud tips or "eyes." Plant ginger as you would turmeric, just under the soil surface. In the fall, stop watering and place in a cool location indoors. Plants will lose their leaves and go dormant. The following spring, repot and begin watering. New shoots will grow, and rhizomes will be ready for harvest by the end of summer. Plants will grow to a height of three or four feet.

ANNUAL OR PERENNIAL: Perennial

LIGHT: Prefers morning sun and afternoon shade in hot climates. Plant in full sun in the north.

WATERING: In the summer, water containers daily and raised beds with at least two inches per week. Mist leaves during dry periods to maintain moisture levels.

SOIL: Moist, well-draining, nutrient-rich loamy soil

ZONE: Hardy in zones 9 to 12

PRUNING: Perennial ginger can be divided in the spring. Remove dying leaves.

COMPANIONS: Grow with turmeric, lemongrass, roselle, and cilantro.

HARVESTING: Once foliage has started dying back, lift rhizomes and shake off loose soil. Wash well, remove stems, and allow to dry.

SAFETY CONSIDERATIONS: Food amounts of ginger are considered safe. Stop taking two weeks prior to surgery, as it might slow blood clotting. Don't use it if you have a bleeding disorder.

PRESERVATION: Peel, slice, and dry in a dehydrator set at 120°F. Grind into a fine powder or leave sliced. Store in an airtight glass jar. Ginger can also be frozen.

TIP: Peel ginger with a spoon. Hold the root firmly and run the edge of a spoon over the flesh. It will come off easily and prevent waste.

KEEP IN MIND: Pre-sprout ginger by placing it in a dark cupboard. After several weeks, shoots will appear, giving you a head start on planting.

TROUBLESHOOTING: Container-grown ginger will produce a smaller harvest in cooler areas. Grow several containers to achieve a larger crop.

LICORICE

(Glycyrrhiza glabra)

Common name(s): licorice, sweet root

PARTS USED: Roots

USES: Licorice root contains a substance called glycyrrhizin, which is fifty times sweeter than sucrose. It is often added to herbal tea blends for natural sweetness. Simmer in a decoction for fifteen minutes and enjoy as tea.

Licorice has many medicinal benefits and may be used to support digestion, soothe a sore throat, reduce heartburn, and treat bacterial infections. Licorice tea is thirst-quenching.

TASTE PROFILE: Anise, fennel, sweet, slightly bitter

GROWING: Licorice is an herbaceous perennial that dies to the ground over winter. Although licorice may be grown from seed, it will take at least three years for a plant to establish. If possible, purchase nursery-grown plants to achieve a quicker harvest. Licorice is best grown directly in the garden, where it will have more space to establish and set down roots. If you live in a zone lower than 7, consider planting it in a large container and moving it indoors or into a heated greenhouse for the winter. Licorice will grow to a height of two to six feet.

ANNUAL OR PERENNIAL: Perennial

LIGHT: Prefers full sun

WATERING: A minimum of two inches of water per week

SOIL: Well-draining, nutrient-rich, sandy to loamy soil. Avoid planting in clay soil.

ZONE: Hardy in zones 7 to 10

PRUNING: No pruning required unless dividing established plants.

COMPANIONS: Plant with sweet violets and rosemary. Don't plant with brassicas and alliums.

HARVESTING: Harvest licorice in the fall by pulling up the plant. Shake off excess soil and wash with a stiff brush under running water.

SAFETY CONSIDERATIONS: It is unsafe to take licorice during pregnancy because it may cause miscarriage or an early delivery. Avoid using it if breastfeeding, due to a lack of research showing it is safe. Licorice may interact with blood thinners, and if you take large amounts of licorice, it may cause headaches, bloating, and raised blood pressure. Licorice may act as an estrogen in the body; don't take it if you have a hormone-sensitive condition. Stop using two weeks prior to surgery.

PRESERVATION: Cut cleaned roots into pieces with a knife or scissors and dehydrate at 140°F to 150°F until hard. Store in an airtight glass jar away from direct sunlight.

TIP: *Glycyrrhiza glabra* is different from *Helichrysum petiolare*, which is often confused with the licorice plant. It is best to refer to the botanical name when purchasing plants.

KEEP IN MIND: Flowering is not required to achieve a harvest.

TROUBLESHOOTING: Licorice has deep taproots and rhizomes. Upon harvesting, if any roots remain in the soil, they will grow back the following year. Choose a long-term location away from other plants, because licorice is difficult to eliminate.

TURMERIC

(Curcuma longa)

Common name(s): turmeric

PARTS USED: Roots and leaves

USES: Turmeric root and leaves are commonly used in Indian and Asian cooking. Turmeric also makes a lovely tea. Add dry turmeric powder to tea blends for its powerful health benefits. Make a golden milk latte with turmeric powder.

The curcumin in turmeric has strong antioxidant properties and is antibacterial when applied topically. Turmeric is used to help with digestion, supports the immune system, is anti-inflammatory, lowers triglycerides, and is often used to support osteoarthritis.

TASTE PROFILE: Mildly bitter, earthy, slightly sweet, and astringent

GROWING: Where turmeric is perennial, grow in a raised bed or large container garden. Turmeric cannot drop below 50°F and should be grown as an annual or grown in a pot, then brought indoors for the winter. Start pot-grown turmeric in the late winter from organic store-bought rhizomes. Select rhizomes with established “eyes” or buds. Lay rhizomes on the soil surface, spaced three inches apart, and cover with a one-inch layer of soil, then water well. When all danger of frost has passed, set pots outside and water daily. Turmeric can grow to a height of three or four feet. It will take at least nine months to achieve a good harvest.

ANNUAL OR PERENNIAL: Perennial in warm regions

LIGHT: Prefers a partially sunny location in hot climates. Plant in full sun in the north.

WATERING: Water container-grown turmeric daily. Provide two inches of water per week if grown in a raised bed.

SOIL: Well-draining, loamy soil, rich in organic matter

ZONE: Hardy in zones 8 to 10; grow as an annual in lower hardiness zones.

PRUNING: In a perennial garden, divide rhizomes each spring. Remove any dead leaves as they appear.

COMPANIONS: Grow with pole beans or peas to cast shade. Ginger has similar growing requirements.

HARVESTING: When leaves start to die back, dig up the plant, shake off excess soil, and rinse well. Remove green shoots and allow to air-dry.

SAFETY CONSIDERATIONS: Pregnant and breastfeeding women shouldn't take medicinal amounts of turmeric. Do not take it if you have a gallbladder problem or a bleeding disorder. Stop using turmeric two weeks before surgery.

PRESERVATION: Turmeric may be peeled, sliced, and dehydrated at 120°F until hard. Grind in a coffee grinder until a fine powder. Store in a dark cupboard, in an airtight glass jar.

TIP: Purchase organic turmeric for planting, as regular turmeric may be sprayed with a sprouting inhibitor.

KEEP IN MIND: Turmeric will stain your hands, clothes, and countertop when cut. Prepare your hands and surface before using.

TROUBLESHOOTING: An overly sunny and hot location will scorch plant leaves and dry the soil. Where summers are hot, mist leaves daily to maintain humidity and moisture.

CHAPTER 7

Tea Blend Recipes

In this chapter, you will find recipes that use some of the plant profiles provided in the previous chapters.

REST AND RELAX TEA

MAKES 4 cups loose tea (96 cups brewed tea)

This tea will calm the stomach and the mind. Drink a cup before bed or after a heavy meal. This tea can help relieve bloating, gas, and indigestion.

2 cups dried chamomile flowers
1 cup dried mint
½ cup dried lavender flowers
½ cup dried sweet violet flowers
Honey, for sweetening (optional)

In a large bowl or glass measuring cup, combine the chamomile, mint, lavender, and sweet violets. Mix well and transfer the tea to a large airtight glass jar. Label with the ingredients and instructions for use.

TO USE: Boil water to 203°F. Measure 2 teaspoons of the tea blend into a large tea infuser or tea bag. Steep the tea in 8 ounces of water for 10 to 15 minutes. Strain and drink 1 cup as needed. Sweeten with honey (if using).

VARIATIONS: If you don't have sweet violets, you can omit them altogether. Lavender may be omitted if you have a sensitivity to it. Substitute anise hyssop for either one.

STORAGE: Store the tea blend in a dark cupboard or pantry for one to two years.

SAFETY INFORMATION: Pregnant and breastfeeding women should avoid drinking large amounts of this tea. The chamomile in the tea may interact if taking blood thinners. For some, lavender may cause constipation, headache, or skin irritation.

HEALTH AND WELLNESS TEA

MAKES 2¾ cups loose tea (66 cups brewed tea)

Drink this tea for its immune-boosting, digestion-easing, and anti-inflammatory properties. Calendula is a powerful antioxidant, anti-inflammatory, antimicrobial, and antifungal that can help soothe a sore throat and relieve congested lymph nodes, and mint can freshen breath and help relieve a tension headache.

1½ cups dried mint
½ cup dried calendula petals
½ cup fennel seeds
¼ cup dried ginger root
Honey, for sweetening (optional)

In a medium bowl or glass measuring cup, combine the mint, calendula, fennel, and ginger. Mix well and transfer the tea to an airtight glass jar. Label with the ingredients and instructions for use.

TO USE: Boil water to 203°F. Measure 2 teaspoons of the tea blend into a large tea infuser. Steep covered for 10 to 20 minutes in 8 ounces of water. Strain and sweeten with honey (if using). Drink no more than 2 or 3 cups per day.

VARIATIONS: You can substitute anise seeds or dried anise leaves if you don't have fennel.

STORAGE: Store the tea blend in a dark cupboard for up to two years.

SAFETY INFORMATION: Pregnant women shouldn't drink this tea, because calendula can stimulate menstruation. Ginger should be avoided if you have a bleeding disorder. Stop drinking this tea two weeks prior to surgery. Large amounts of mint should be avoided by pregnant and nursing women.

REFRESHING CITRUS TEA

MAKES 2½ cups loose tea (60 cups brewed tea)

Drink this tea hot or iced on a warm, sunny day. The lemon and roselle add a bright, citrus flavor to this delicious red tea.

1 cup dried roselle
½ cup dried anise hyssop
½ cup dried lemon verbena leaves
¼ cup dried lemon peel
¼ cup dried calendula petals

In a medium bowl or glass measuring cup, combine the roselle, anise hyssop, lemon verbena, lemon peel, and calendula. Mix well and transfer the tea to an airtight glass jar. Label with the ingredients and instructions for use.

TO USE: Boil water to 203°F. Measure 2 teaspoons of the tea blend and steep in 8 ounces of water in a large tea infuser or tea bag for 10 minutes. Strain and drink hot or fill a large glass halfway with ice and pour the tea over top. Stir and enjoy! Drink no more than 2 or 3 cups per day.

VARIATIONS: If you don't have lemon verbena, substitute lemongrass. A squeeze of fresh lemon into iced tea will add a stronger lemon flavor.

STORAGE: Store the tea blend in a dark cupboard or pantry for up to one year.

SAFETY INFORMATION: Pregnant women shouldn't drink this tea because calendula can stimulate menstruation. Anise hyssop can cause uterine contractions, potentially leading to miscarriage. Lemon verbena can irritate the kidneys, so don't take it if you have kidney problems. Stop taking this tea at least two weeks prior to surgery.

ENERGY TEA

MAKES 2½ cups loose tea (60 cups brewed tea)

A cup of energy tea contains herbs that will help boost your immune system, calm your mind, reduce stress levels, and relieve headaches. Drink it after a meal to help with digestion.

1 cup dried mint
½ cup dried lemongrass leaves
½ cup dried lemon balm
¼ cup ginger root
¼ cup turmeric root
Honey, for sweetening (optional)

Combine the mint, lemongrass, lemon balm, ginger, and turmeric in a large glass measuring cup or bowl. Mix well and transfer the tea to an airtight glass jar. Label with the ingredients and instructions for use.

TO USE: Boil water to 203°F. Measure 2 teaspoons of the tea blend into a tea infuser. Steep covered for 15 to 20 minutes in 8 ounces of water. Strain, then sweeten with honey (if using). Drink 1 or 2 cups as needed.

VARIATIONS: Turmeric has a strong flavor. Omit if preferred. Squeeze in half a lemon to enhance the lemony notes.

STORAGE: Store the tea blend in a dark cupboard or pantry for up to two years.

SAFETY INFORMATION: Pregnant and nursing women shouldn't drink this tea. Lemongrass may start menstrual flow. Ginger and turmeric should be avoided if you have a bleeding disorder. Avoid lemon balm if you have thyroid disease. Stop drinking this tea at least two weeks prior to surgery.

HERBAL BEDTIME TEA

MAKES 4 cups loose tea (96 cups brewed tea)

Add this tea to your bedtime routine, and it will help relax you for a good night's rest.

1½ cups dried chamomile flowers
1 cup dried lemon balm, crushed
½ cup dried catnip, crushed
½ cup dried oat straw
½ cup dried passionflowers
¼ cup dried hops, crushed
Honey, for sweetening (optional)

In a large bowl or glass measuring cup, combine the chamomile, lemon balm, catnip, oat straw, passionflowers, and hops. Mix well and transfer the tea to an airtight glass jar. Label with the ingredients and instructions for use.

TO USE: To brew the tea, use 1 tablespoon of the herbal blend per cup, and place it in a tea ball or infuser. In a mug, pour water boiled to 203°F over the herbs and steep for 15 minutes. Sweeten with honey (if using). Drink 1 cup of this tea each night before bed.

STORAGE: Store the tea in a cool, dry place for up to two years.

TUMMY TAMER TEA

MAKES 2 cups loose tea (48 cups brewed tea)

A tea to enjoy after a heavy meal; drink this tea to help soothe the stomach and relieve gas or bloating pain.

1 cup dried mint
½ cup dried chamomile
¼ cup dried basil or tulsi basil
¼ cup fennel seeds

In a small bowl, combine the mint, chamomile, basil, and fennel. Mix well, and transfer the tea to an airtight container. Label with the ingredients and instructions for use.

TO USE: Steep 2 teaspoons of the tea blend in 8 ounces of water boiled to 203°F for 20 to 25 minutes. Drink ½ cup to 1 cup as needed.

STORAGE: Store the tea blend in a cool, dark location for up to two years.

SAFETY INFORMATION: Large amounts of mint should be avoided by pregnant and nursing women. Large therapeutic doses of fennel could cause nervousness and complications in pregnancy.

Resources

Books

Farrell, Holly. *The Kew Gardener's Guide to Growing Herbs*. London, UK: Frances Lincoln, 2019. A beautifully illustrated guide on growing your own herbs. Each section is categorized by project and their subsequent herbs.

Gladstar, Rosemary. *Rosemary Gladstar's Herbal Recipes for Vibrant Health*. North Adams, MA: Storey Publishing, 2008. A comprehensive guide to growing and ecologically harvesting herbs, then using them to prepare herbal remedies. Many herbal tea recipes are included in this book.

Houdret, Jessica. *The Complete Book of Herbs and Herb Gardening*. London, UK: Hermes House, 2009. A comprehensive guide from A to Z on growing and using herbs.

Websites

Herbal Academy, TheHerbalAcademy.com. This site has herbalism courses, workshops, recipes, and more.

Richters Herbs, Richters.com. This seed company has the widest selection of herbs you will find, including many rare herbs. Order a free catalog, which includes uses and growing information for each seed.

The Seed Starting Calculator, JuliaDimakos.com/Seed-Starting-Calculator. Enter your final frost date and the calculator will tell you exactly when to start your herb, vegetable, and flower seeds, along with growing tips.

West Coast Seeds, WestCoastSeeds.com. A website to find many herb and flower seeds, along with growing tips and information.

References

Boros, Klára, Nikoletta Jedlinszki, and Dezső Csupor. "Theanine and Caffeine Content of Infusions Prepared from Commercial Tea Samples." *Pharmacognosy Magazine* 12, no. 45 (2016): 75–79. ncbi.nlm.nih.gov/pmc/articles/PMC4787341.

Gascoyne, Kevin, Francois Marchand, and Jasmin Desharnais. *Tea: History, Terroirs, Varieties*. Buffalo, NY: Firefly Books Ltd, 2018.

Gladstar, Rosemary. *Rosemary Gladstar's Medicinal Herbs. A Beginner's Guide.* North Adams, MA: Storey Publishing, 2012.

Hahn, Jeff, et al. "Spotted wing drosophila." Reviewed in 2020. University of Minnesota Extension. Accessed February 2020. extension.umn.edu/yard-and-garden-insects/spotted-wing-drosophila.

Hicks, Monique, Y-H. Peggy Hsieh, and Leonard N. Bell. "Tea Preparation and Its Influence on Methylxanthine Concentration." *Food Research International* 29, nos. 3–4 (April–May 1996): 325–30. Accessed Jan 17, 2022. sciencedirect.com/science/article/abs/pii/0963996996000385.

Higdon, Jane. "Tea." Oregon State University, Linus Pauling Institute: Micronutrient Information Center. Last modified October 2015. lpi.oregonstate.edu/mic/food-beverages/tea.

Kluepfel, Marjan, and Bob Lippert. "Changing the pH of Your Soil." Home & Garden Information Center. Last modified October 20, 2012. hgic.clemson.edu/factsheet/changing-the-ph-of-your-soil/#:~:text=Vegetables%2C%20grasses%20and%20most%20ornamentals,vigorous%20growth%20and%20nutrient%20deficiencies.

Lima, Patrick. *Herbs: The Complete Gardener's Guide.* Buffalo, NY: Firefly Books, 2012.

Liversidge, Cassie. *Homegrown Tea: An Illustrated Guide to Planting, Harvesting and Blending Teas and Tisanes.* New York: St. Martin's Press, 2014.

McVicar, Jekka. *Jekka's Complete Herb Book.* London, UK: Kyle Books, 2007.

Metropulos, Megan. "What Are the Health Benefits of Oolong Tea?" *MedicalNews Today*. September 6, 2017. medicalnewstoday.com/articles/319276#potential-health-benefits-of-oolong-tea.

Missouri Botanical Garden. "*Agastache foeniculum*." n.d. Accessed February 2022. missouribotanicalgarden.org/PlantFinder/PlantFinderDetails.aspx?taxonid=281382&isprofile=1&basic=anise%20hyssop.

Missouri Botanical Garden. "Ribes nigrum 'Ben Sarek'." n.d. Accessed February 2022. missouribotanicalgarden.org/PlantFinder/PlantFinderDetails.aspx?taxonid=257221&isprofile=0&pt=7.

Missouri Botanical Garden. "*Rosa Rugosa*." n.d. Accessed February 2022. missouribotanicalgarden.org/PlantFinder/PlantFinderDetails.aspx?taxonid=286364.

Missouri Botanical Garden. "*Vaccinium corymbosum*." n.d. Accessed February 2022. missouribotanicalgarden.org/PlantFinder/PlantFinderDetails.aspx?taxonid=279992&isprofile=1&basic=Vaccinium%20corymbosum.

Morton, Julia. "Fruits of Warm Climates." Accessed February 2022. hort.purdue.edu/newcrop/morton/index.html.

North Carolina Extension Gardener Plant Toolbox. n.d. Accessed February 2022. plants.ces.ncsu.edu.

Perry, Leonard. "Homegrown Teas." *Green Mountain Gardener*. pss.uvm.edu/ppp/articles/teatime.html.

Söhle, Jörn, Anja Knott, Ursula Holtzmann, Ralf Siegner, Elke Grönniger, Andreas Schepky, Stefan Gallinat, Horst Wenck, Franz Stäb, and Marc Winnefeld. "White Tea Extract Induces Lipolytic Activity and Inhibits Adipogenesis in Human Subcutaneous (Pre)-Adipocytes." *Nutrition & Metabolism* 6, no. 20 (May 2009). Accessed February 2022. pubmed.ncbi.nlm.nih.gov/19409077.

Sundberg, Maureen. "Rainwater for Gardens: Why Plants Love Rainwater Best." Ecological Landscape Alliance. August 15, 2016. ecolandscaping.org/08/developing-healthy-landscapes/ecological-landscaping-101/rainwater-for-gardens-why-plants-love-rainwater-best.

UF|IFAS Gardening Solutions, University of Florida. "Camellia Pests and Problems." Last modified December 6, 2021. gardeningsolutions.ifas.ufl.edu/care/pests-and-diseases/pests/camellia-pests-and-problems.html.

UK Tea & Infusions Association. "The History of Tea." Accessed January 2022. tea.co.uk/history-of-tea.

USDA Plant Hardiness Zone Map. n.d. Accessed February 2022. planthardiness.ars.usda.gov.

Weisenhorn, Julie. "Edible Flowers." Reviewed 2018. University of Minnesota Extension. Accessed February 2022. extension.umn.edu/flowers/edible-flowers#sources-752610.

Index

G

H

I

L

M

O

P

R

S

T

W

Acknowledgments

Thank you to my husband, Stelios, for your constant support of my gardening projects and for helping me accomplish my dreams. To my children, Georgia and Ilias, for your patience and understanding while I worked long hours meeting deadlines for this book. To the publishing team at Callisto Media, thank you for this opportunity. It has been a pleasure! Special thanks to Anne and Vanessa.

About the Author

Julia Dimakos has been growing food for over eleven years. In 2018, Julia expanded her kitchen garden from two thousand to seven thousand square feet, giving her more space to grow the vegetables, herbs, and flowers that she loves.

Julia is known as "The Gardening Girl" and can be found on Instagram @juliadimakos, YouTube at youtube.com/gardeninggirl, and Facebook @juliadimakos2. She has been writing about growing food since 2013 and can be found at her blog, JuliaDimakos.com. She is a regular speaker at horticultural societies and loves sharing her knowledge. Julia lives in Mono, Ontario, Canada on twenty-five acres with her husband, Stelios, her children, Georgia and Ilias, and their cat, Vasya.

Printed in the USA
CPSIA information can be obtained
at www.ICGtesting.com
CBHW040038200324
5545CB00002B/11